Anticipating Ethnic Conflict

Ashley J. Tellis • Thomas S. Szayna • James A. Winnefeld

Prepared for the United States Army

RAND | Arroyo Center

PREFACE

This report provides a handbook for intelligence analysts to use in thinking about and attempting to anticipate the occurrence of ethnic conflict. The intended audience and users of the handbook are Army intelligence analysts, though analysts from other intelligence agencies also should find it useful. The handbook is formatted as a series of questions and guidelines for the analyst to focus on while preparing an assessment. The questions are based on a conceptual model of ethnic and communitarian strife that focuses on the processes of grievance formation and group mobilization.

This document is the final product of a project entitled "Ethnic Conflict and the Processes of State Breakdown: Improving Army Planning and Preparation." The project aimed to improve the Army's ability to anticipate ethnic conflict as one aspect of its overall strategic planning and threat assessment. The academic audience will be especially interested in the appendix, whereas the more practically oriented audience may find the handbook of greater interest. The two are provided here because the publication attempts to combine them in order to provide a theoretically grounded tool for practical use.

The research was sponsored by the Deputy Chief of Staff for Intelligence, U.S. Army, and was conducted in the Strategy and Doctrine Program of RAND's Arroyo Center. The Arroyo Center is a federally funded research and development center sponsored by the United States Army.

CONTENTS

FIGURES

TABLES

SUMMARY

This document provides a practical tool—a guidebook and a methodology to follow—for intelligence analysts to use in determining the long-term potential for communitarian and ethnic conflict. It is based on a deductive model of group conflict. The model is not a mechanistic tool, but a heuristic device with a threefold purpose:

- To order the analyst's thinking about the logic and dynamics of potential ethnically based violence and to aid in defining the information-collection requirements of such an analysis;
- To provide a general conceptual framework about how ethnic grievances form and group mobilization occurs and how these processes could lead to violence under certain conditions; and
- To assist the intelligence community with the long-range assessment of possible ethnic strife.

The framework presented here is not meant to substitute for the knowledge, reasoning, or judgment of intelligence analysts. It is simply a tool to help them order the information already at their command (and to identify the information they still need) as they attempt to assess the prospects for ethnic strife.

The three-stage model traces the development of ethnic and communitarian strife, beginning with the conditions that may lead to the formation of an ethnic group, then the group's mobilization for political action, and ultimately its competition with the state. Keeping in mind that the goal is to provide a tool for intelligence analysts to use when assessing whether a competition between an ethnic group and the state will end in violence, the model provides a series of matrices to help the analyst identify the conditions that may lead to ethnic and communitarian strife. The crucial part of the model is that the *interaction* between the group and the state determines the outcome. The preferences of the group and the state for violence or accommodation depend on their strengths and weaknesses *relative* to each other.

The model contributes in a number of ways to our ability to think more rigorously about the development of ethnic and communitarian strife. First, it characterizes human behavior in collectivities as rational and as a phenomenon that can be understood. Accordingly, it treats the current wave of communal strife simply as a type of social and political competition. Second, the framework does not treat ethnicity as some kind of a given but as a constructed social phenomenon. Ethnicity, as used here, refers to the idea of shared group affinity and a sense of belonging that is based on a myth of collective ancestry and a notion of distinctiveness. The group in question must be larger than a kinship group, but its cohesion stems from constructed bonds that have similarities to kinship. The constructed bonds may be grounded in any number of distinguishing cultural or physical characteristics, such as common language, religion, or regional differentiation; they are incidental and case-specific. Third, the framework treats ethnic action as a subset of political action; as such, ethnic action does not occur spontaneously but requires mobilization and direction.

The handbook details the specific steps that the analyst might follow in determining a society's long-term potential for ethnic and communitarian strife. The theoretical foundation for the contents of the handbook is provided in the appendix. This discussion is drawn from social-science (especially political science, sociology, and economics) discussions of the past several decades, especially as developed in the subfields of rational choice theory, ethnicity and nationalism, and collective violence. The theoretical discussion integrates the diverse insights offered by various theories that focus on separate aspects of ethnic and communitarian strife—such as relative deprivation of the populace or the extent of state capacity—into a comprehensive model that speaks to the entire *process* of ethnic mobilization, from the structural roots of conflict all the way to social reconciliation or state breakdown.

The framework presented here is tailored to intelligence audiences in general and to Army intelligence in particular as they address the problem of the increasing use of the U.S. Army in peacekeeping interventions in the post–Cold War era. Most of the Army's experiences in this realm have involved intrastate ethnic or communitarian conflicts. Increasingly, it appears that many of the conflicts the U.S. Army will confront in the foreseeable future will be intrastate operations, with traditional major regional conflicts (MRCs) becoming the exception to the rule. Better anticipation of such strife may lead to improvements in the Army's training, equipping, doctrine and deployment. Equally important, however, better anticipation of ethnic communitarian strife may allow remedial action to be taken preemptively rather than reactively, perhaps by political institutions instead of military means.

ACKNOWLEDGMENTS

We are deeply grateful to Donald Horowitz of Duke University and Robert Dorff of the Army War College for their thorough and extremely helpful reviews of this document. We also thank Daniel Byman at RAND for his time and effort in the review process. Special thanks are due to Marten Van Heuven, Graham Fuller, and Tom McNaugher at RAND for their contributions and comments on earlier drafts of this document. Finally, Nikki Shacklett performed the difficult task of editing the manuscript.

Chapter One

INTRODUCTION

Communitarian strife at the substate level, often dubbed "ethnic conflict," has gained much attention in the aftermath of the Cold War. Despite its higher prominence, however, the phenomenon of ethnic conflict is not new. Historically, major world events such as decolonization, the collapse of empires, and, more recently, the collapse of communism have caused spikes in the incidence of ethnic conflict. But communitarian and ethnic conflicts at the substate level have been with us throughout the 20th century.[1] A steady increase in the number of states in the world and growing social pressures associated with modernization suggest that communitarian and ethnic conflicts will remain with us for a long time. Such strife may even increase in the years ahead.

This report is the final product of a year-long project entitled "Ethnic Conflict and the Processes of State Breakdown: Improving Army Planning and Preparation," which sought to help Army intelligence analysts who monitor intrastate (including ethnically based) conflict potential around the world. The work of these analysts has grown more important since the end of the Cold War, as the U.S. Army has become increasingly engaged in peacekeeping and peace enforcement operations aimed at preventing, quelling, or dealing with the consequences of ethnic or communitarian strife in Somalia, Rwanda, Macedonia, and Bosnia-Herzegovina. Facing the serious prospect of further involvement in such conflicts in the years ahead, the Army

[1]See the appendix in Roy Licklider, "The Consequences of Negotiated Settlements in Civil Wars, 1945–1993," *American Political Science Review*, Vol. 89, No. 3 (September 1995), pp. 681–690.

has to grapple with the problem of what such intrastate operations imply for its training, equipping, doctrine, and deployment.[2] While the primary mission of the Army and the U.S. armed forces in general will remain the fighting of wars and protecting U.S. interests in the world, peace operations (ranging from traditional peacekeeping, to peace enforcement, to humanitarian assistance) will place increasing demands on the U.S. armed forces in the next 10–15 years, with the Army (and the Marines) most affected. To put it bluntly, there "will be more Somalias, Rwandas, Haitis and Burundis in the future,"[3] and the Army will be called upon to deal with some of them. Since the end of the Cold War, the Army has been called upon 25 times to conduct peacekeeping and other humanitarian missions and, as the Army Chief of Staff General Dennis Reimer recently noted, "that is a 300 percent increase and that trend is expected to continue."[4]

Equally important, however, a better understanding and anticipation of such conflicts may improve the prospects for preemptive remedial action short of using force. Experience shows that ethnic and communitarian conflicts are difficult to extinguish once started and may result in international crises, either because they have spawned a humanitarian disaster or because another country has exploited the internal strife for its own purposes. Ethnic bonds are psychologically similar to kinship bonds and involve issues of identity. Individuals and groups with deeply internalized ethnic bonds (sometimes to the point of seeing them as immutable) may develop almost fanatical personal attachments to the cause. Thus it is no accident that many ethnic and communitarian conflicts end up in prolonged and bloody strife, sometimes mixed in with attempts at genocide and complete

---

[2]For a survey of these issues, see James A. Winnefeld et al., *Intervention in Intrastate Conflict: Implications for the Army in the Post–Cold War Era,* Santa Monica, CA: RAND, MR-554/1-A, 1995.

[3]Walter Clarke and Robert Gosende, "Keeping the Mission Focused: The Intelligence Component in Peace Operations," *Defense Intelligence Journal*, Vol. 5, No. 2 (Fall 1996), pp. 47–69.

[4]Comments by General Dennis Reimer to the U.S. Senate, *Defense Daily,* April 17, 1997, p. 105. To illustrate the point further, during the eight post–Cold War years (1989–1996) there were 101 armed conflicts, of which only six were interstate conflicts. Peter Wallensteen and Margareta Sollenberg, "Armed Conflicts, Conflict Termination and Peace Agreements, 1989–96," *Journal of Peace Research,* Vol. 34, No. 3 (1997), pp. 339–358.

elimination of the other side.[5] All these considerations suggest the United States would be better served if it could prevent the evolution of communitarian and ethnic tensions into outright strife.[6]

The U.S. intelligence community has a mixed record when it comes to anticipating communal violence. Few predicted the recent rapid disintegration of Rwanda into genocide, for example. Even when accurate intelligence forecasts were available, such as on the former Yugoslavia, important elements of the conflict's driving forces were largely unexpected. In both cases, widespread outrage and disgust over atrocities have led to the deployment of U.S. Army units to try to ameliorate some of the consequent suffering.

This project sought to improve the Army's intelligence assessment by providing a theoretical model of the social processes and dynamics that lead to ethnic and communitarian conflict and state breakdown. Under what conditions are ethnic groups likely to take up violence against the state in order to accomplish their goals? When are they more likely to favor the peaceful pursuit of group aims? Similarly, under what conditions are states likely to resort to violence and repression as opposed to negotiation with the aggrieved group? Put more simply, the project sought to draw on existing scholarly knowledge about the evolution of communitarian and ethnic conflict to produce a practical tool for analysts and policymakers. In a larger

---

[5]As many scholars and analysts have noted, ethnic conflict is a type of social competition that "typically involve[s] large amounts of violence and often particularly vicious forms of violence." Samuel Huntington, "Civil Violence and the Process of Development," in *Civil Violence and the International System*, Adelphi Paper 83, London: IISS, 1971, p. 13. Ethnicity has not been the main aspect of the genocides and mass murders in the 20th century. Instead, state-sponsored and ideologically motivated mass murders (USSR, China, Cambodia) have been by far the worst incidents. However, studies have shown that civil wars (sometimes with an ethnic dimension) have provided the opportunity structure for state-sponsored genocides. See Matthew Krain, "State-Sponsored Mass Murder: The Onset and Severity of Genocides and Politicides," *Journal of Conflict Resolution*, Vol. 41, No. 3 (June 1997), pp. 331–360.

[6]It is at least partly in response to the demands placed upon the U.S. armed forces that interest in conflict prevention has appeared in such strength in recent years. For some good recent literature, see David A. Lake and Donald Rothchild, "Containing Fear: The Origins and Management of Ethnic Conflict," *International Security*, Vol. 21, No. 2 (Fall 1996), pp. 41–75; and William J. Dixon, "Third-party Techniques for Preventing Conflict Escalation and Promoting Peaceful Settlement," *International Organization*, Vol. 50, No. 4 (Autumn 1996), pp. 653–681.

sense, the project aimed to improve the Army's ability to identify and plan for potential ethnic conflict contingencies around the world as well as to contribute to interagency planning for such contingencies.

This document represents the final product of the project. It is designed to be used as a handbook and practical guide for intelligence analysts as they face the possibilities of intrastate communitarian and ethnic conflict around the world. Thus, it is intended as a contribution to the stepped-up efforts by the intelligence community to come up with better tools to anticipate ethnic conflict.[7]

The theoretical model proposed here differs from most of the intelligence community's existing aids that the authors are aware of. The aids most commonly used seem to take the form of large-scale inductive models that statistically "grind up" enormous amounts of data, ranging from health and mortality statistics to the number of individuals under arms, in an effort to develop useful predictors of political violence.[8] Such predictors, if at all finally available, merely describe correlations between some class of data and political violence. They do not establish a *causal* link between the variables included and the social outcome they seek to explain. Not surprisingly, such inductive models cannot ask questions that bear on the problem of *how* deprivation and discontent lead to strife. Thus they cannot generate a targeted set of information requirements that intelligence agencies can pursue to increase the understanding of causes and the ability to predict with respect to the problem of ethnic violence.

In contrast, the methodology in this report seeks to elucidate how ethnic attachments are channeled into political action that may re-

---

[7]For example, the journal of the Defense Intelligence College has given considerable space to the problem; for example, see the articles in the section "Ethnic Conflict—Threat to U.S. National Security?" *Defense Intelligence Journal*, Vol. 1, No. 2 (Fall 1992). Classroom hours devoted to operations other than war for intelligence officers have risen sharply since 1990 for all of the services as well as for the DIA (a 73 percent increase for the Army between 1990 and 1995). Stephen L. Caldwell, "Defense Intelligence Training: Changing to Better Support the Warfighter," *Defense Intelligence Journal*, Vol. 4, No. 2 (Fall 1995), pp. 83–100.

[8]The authors emphasize the caveat that this is their impression based on their awareness of the problem. For references to some of the models, see Pauline H. Baker and John A. Ausink, "State Collapse and Ethnic Violence: Toward a Predictive Model," *Parameters*, Spring 1996, pp. 19–31.

sult in strife. It incorporates insights from a variety of theories—relative deprivation, for example, and state capacity models—into a more comprehensive structure covering the entire *process* of ethnic mobilization. The result is not a "model" in the standard (mechanistic) sense used by intelligence analysts, but rather a method in the tradition of scientific inquiry that aims to explore the basic structure and processes of a given phenomenon. It is, emphatically, not meant to be a mechanistic substitute for the knowledge, reasoning, and judgment of intelligence analysts, but rather a means for helping them order the information already at their command (and identify important information gaps) as they attempt to assess the prospects for ethnic strife.

The primary goal of the theoretical model and the handbook is to help the intelligence community with *long-range assessments of possible ethnic strife,* as opposed to forecasts of imminent ethnic violence and ethnic breakdown. Incorporating the level of detail needed to adequately predict imminent violence under a variety of conditions would call for more finely grained explanations and would be useful for intelligence analysts whose task is to monitor day-to-day flows of events. However, such models by definition would presume that ethnically driven competition is already under way, so they would be less useful for assessing when and under what conditions ethnic mobilization may in fact come about (just the kind of work that forms the staple of analyses focusing on various long-range futures facing a given state or region). It is also important to recognize that, for a variety of theoretical reasons, it is probably impossible to develop any single model that can explain imminent ethnic breakdown. Such a task would most likely require multiple models, and they would vary according to the outcomes to be explained (for example, mass refugee movements, ethnic violence, genocide, and state collapse would each require separate models) and the relative weights assigned to various remote causes, proximate causes, and event sequences that combine to produce such outcomes.

ASSUMPTIONS AND CONSIDERATIONS

There are several considerations and assumptions underlying the theoretical model and the handbook based on it. To begin with, and in line with the fundamental assumptions of modern social science, the model assumes that human behavior in collectivities is rational and can be understood. This contrasts sharply with the popular perception of ethnic conflict as primitive, atavistic, and irrational. If human behavior is irrational, it cannot be predicted or even anticipated. If, on the other hand, the current wave of communal strife fits into the general category of social and political competition, its dynamics may indeed be understandable, and so more effective anticipation of ethnic conflict may be possible. Rationality should not be understood as a universally agreed-upon mindset but a recognition that individuals have goals and will attempt to reach them by what they see as the easiest and least costly (or most efficient) means. The rationality assumption does not mean that all individuals have the same goals. But if an individual's goals are understood, then his actions should be predictable in principle.

The model also assumes that ethnicity is not some kind of a given, but rather is a constructed social phenomenon. As used here, ethnicity refers to the idea of shared group affinity and a sense of belonging that is based on a myth of collective ancestry and a notion of distinctiveness. The group in question must be larger than a kinship group, but the myth-engendered sense of belonging to the group stems from constructed bonds that have similarities to kinship. Psychologically, for the individual, the ethnic group is the largest extension of the family. The constructed bonds of ethnicity may stem from any number of distinguishing cultural or physical characteristics, such as common language, religion, or regional differentiation. As a form of constructed identity, ethnicity is more malleable than is often assumed. It is also more ephemeral: it must be continually created and recreated through a multitude of socialization processes. Although ethnic activists often claim that ethnicity is somehow predetermined, it is difficult to subscribe to this claim from a rationalist perspective. However, ethnic attachments are no less real for being socially constructed, and, indeed, ethnic attachments may elicit intense loyalty.

The construction of ethnicity is a by-product of politics, with politics understood as that activity relating to the production of order in social life. Politics forces individuals to discover common resources in their struggle for survival, and the construction of strong bonds based on perceived shared traits amounts to just such a resource, as the bonds then lead to the creation of an "in group" in the ongoing political struggle. Modernization acts as a catalyst for the process of constructing ethnicity, since it forces individuals to operate in a larger social environment than traditional society. In a traditional society, where an individual's "world" is geographically and psychologically limited, bonds based on kinship are sufficient. But when an individual has to deal with impersonal state and market structures and the larger "world" of the state or province, the old bonds no longer suffice. Then ethnicity becomes a useful resource for an individual in his attempt to survive and prosper in a larger social sphere. And in addition to promoting ethnicity, modernization acts as a catalyst to ethnic tensions through homogenization of values and expectations. As socialization processes become more uniform, all individuals begin to value the same things, such as wealth, political prominence, and social recognition. Thus, they are brought into conflict with other individuals and ethnic groups over the same bones of contention.

By the same token, ethnicity can be a useful tool for political mobilization. Indeed, the model assumes that ethnic action does not occur spontaneously but rather requires mobilization and direction. This assumption runs against the popular image of a disadvantaged group rebelling spontaneously against state tyranny—a romantic image not borne out in reality. There are many examples of severe group deprivation and repression that do not lead to rebellion because the group is not mobilized for political action. Without mobilization, ethnic attachments and feelings may exist but do not have larger political significance.

A final consideration in the theoretical model is its focus on the interaction between a mobilized group and the state as the crucial determinant of strife. In other words, strife does not arise from the group or the state alone, but from the bargaining process between the two. State response to the demands of the mobilized group is just as important as group mobilization in determining whether ethnic tensions will lead to violence. This assumption may seem unexceptional, but it goes against the grain of theoretical analyses that focus primarily on group grievances and group actions.

REPORT ORGANIZATION

This report has two main parts: the handbook and the appendix. The handbook first summarizes the theoretical model of ethnic and communitarian strife and then presents a series of questions to help analysts order and organize the information-collection requirements (on which to base an assessment) into a coherent whole. The handbook explicitly identifies the questions and indicators that an analyst should consider with respect to the various developmental stages of ethnic tensions and strife. It focuses on the characteristics of groups and states most prone to violence so as to help analysts identify them.

The appendix elaborates on the theoretical model that underlies the questions from the handbook portion. It explains in detail the derived results and addresses potential questions about the rationale for inclusion (or lack of inclusion) of certain factors.

Chapter Two

THE MODEL: A SUMMARY

The process leading to ethnic tensions and conflict is divided into three phases: group definition, group mobilization, and strategic bargaining. For the purposes of the intelligence analyst, group definition relates to the structural potential for communitarian strife, group mobilization pertains to the transformation of the potential for strife into likely strife, and strategic bargaining determines whether likely strife will turn into actual strife. Figure 1 illustrates in a graphic format the connections between the three stages of the process.

STAGE 1: THE POTENTIAL FOR STRIFE

Examining the dimensions and characteristics of closure forms the first step in assessing the potential for strife. "Closure" is used here in the Weberian sense as a process of subordination whereby one group monopolizes advantages by closing off opportunities to another group. Given an ascriptive understanding of ethnicity (as defined in Chapter One, with ethnic bonds real but socially constructed on the basis of certain markers), ethnic attachments are a useful resource because they establish an "in group" in the constant struggle for power and domination that comprises politics.

The three arenas of critical importance with respect to closure are the political, the economic, and the social. The political arena relates to all matters of governance, administrative control, and command over the means of coercion. The economic arena relates to all matters connected with the production of wealth and the distribution of resources. The social arena relates to all matters connected with effective claims on social esteem, including the distribution of status

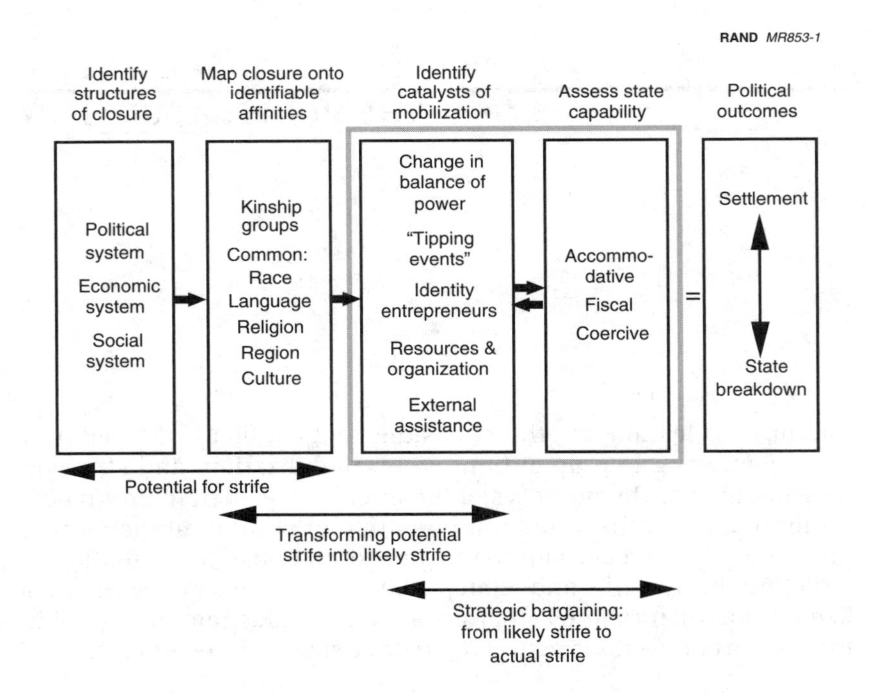

Figure 1—Anticipating Ethnic Conflict

and social privileges. Each of these arenas demarcates a particular dimension of the social order, and each is related in multiple ways to the others, but constrictions in the political realm are perhaps the most important form of closure for the purpose of establishing the potential for strife. The political realm has such primacy because the issue of who rules, and how, directly affects all kinds of outcomes within a polity.

There are two important variables in assessing closure in each of the three arenas: (1) the existing distribution of power, wealth, and status, and (2) the relative ease with which individuals can secure access to power, wealth, and status through peaceful means. The first variable gives a static picture of existing patterns of dominance and deprivation; the second captures the possibilities for peaceful change. But before assessing closure along these two lines, the analyst needs "terms of reference" for the analysis.

Scrutinizing the political, economic, and social arenas does three things: (1) it provides a general profile of which sets of individuals benefit most or are deprived most by the prevailing social structures when classified by certain substatal categories like race, language, religion, region, or culture; (2) it identifies the level of disproportion in the dominance or deprivation of the given group relative to its size or standing in the population as a whole; and (3) it assesses the opportunities for peaceful transformation by means of a systematic scrutiny of the existing institutional structures, the ruling norms of behavior, and the general expectations about appropriate political actions.

Such an examination, conducted skillfully, might suggest whether significant forms of closure exist in any given country.

STAGE 2: TRANSFORMING POTENTIAL STRIFE INTO LIKELY STRIFE

The existence of significant forms of closure does not imply that "ethnic" strife is probable, only that there is some potential for it. Transforming the potential for strife into likely strife requires certain catalytic elements. Indeed, analysts should avoid linking the deprivation experienced by a given population with strife, or even opposition, if the bonds of solidarity among the affected groups are merely latent or fractured. The latter possibility is particularly relevant because modern societies invariably place individuals in multiple roles. As a result, individuals may acquire multiple identities based on the various activities they engage in as well as different levels and kinds of meaning stemming from membership in diverse social formations. There may also be cross-cutting cleavages in society that prevent or ameliorate the coalescence of sharp social divisions despite the existence of otherwise widespread deprivation.

If strife is to move from potential to likely, a catalyst is particularly salient because large-scale social violence rarely if ever occurs as a result of spontaneous social combustion. Such movements need political guidance and organization. In this sense, ethnicity plays a role as an effective tool for mobilization. But the ethnic ingredient does not change the basic fact that all such collective actions simply amount to forms of political mobilization designed to capture power or increase it. Violence that may accompany mobilization is always political violence.

Five factors are critical to understanding the process of how individuals who are potentially motivated as a result of closure and deprivation become mobilized for political action in the form of "ethnic" groups: incipient changes in the balance of power, galvanizing (or "tipping") events, leadership, resources and organization, and foreign assistance.

Incipient changes in the balance of power are recognized alterations in the power relations and closure in a given society. The changes may stem either from long-term trends whose cumulative effect is about to be felt or from sudden events that affect (either negatively or positively) a substate group disproportionately. The critical issue from the point of view of anticipating mobilization is that such changes must be significant in absolute terms and capable of causing major and immediate alterations in the prevailing internal balances of power.

Tipping events are specific events that, under certain conditions, galvanize a group into political action. Any *conspicuous* public events that galvanize group sensibilities, reinforce beliefs in their insular identity, and set off escalating spirals of mutual expectations about collective resistance to the established order can act as tipping events. Tipping events of this sort often become important elements of the historical memory, deepening group identity and accentuating the processes of group formation. They reinforce and clarify the sense of difference and deprivation. They come to serve as the popular symbols of alienation on which individual fears, resentment, and anger all converge—ready to be either molded by interested elites or exploited by interested factions both within the state and outside it.

Leadership (or "identity entrepreneurs" in case of ethnic movements) is a critical factor for political mobilization. Identity entrepreneurs are simply individuals who, for self-interested reasons (and these may range from material and economic to emotional and personality-related), find it profitable to contribute to creating a group identity and bear the costs of mobilizing that group for political action. In ethnic movements they are likely to come from the ranks of the group they are trying to mobilize. Identity entrepreneurs thus help to "create" the ethnic group—if the latter is merely a latent formation up to that point—by "conscientizing"[1] individuals to support certain collective goals as defined by the entrepreneur.

Leadership must be supplemented by resources (financial) and organization. A group's access to resources is in many ways the lifeblood of the mobilization process. It determines the entire nature of mobilization, including the kind of strategy the mobilized group can pursue. Competent organization provides the arteries that channel the lifeblood of resources into effective action. A competent organization is necessary for all kinds of entrepreneurship. For the purposes of large-scale social mobilization, a formal organizational structure (with a hierarchical structure and functional role differentiation) is required.

The final catalyst for effective ethnic mobilization is the possibility of foreign assistance. Strictly speaking, foreign aid to a mobilizing ethnic group is simply another facet of its effort to muster resources. But because such aid pushes domestic power struggles into the realm of interstate competition, the role of foreign agencies and states is best treated as a separate category. A whole set of new issues arises in such situations, as the state authorities can then portray the mobilized ethnic group as a foreign agent and, in turn, claim support from their own allies abroad.

The examination of factors that aid or hinder mobilization serves a single underlying goal: to establish the existence (or absence) of factors that can translate any latent dissatisfaction into political action. The absence of some of the four factors, or variations among them in intensity, will have a direct bearing on the success and extent of mobilization. Whether strife actually occurs, however, does not depend just on the capabilities of the mobilized group. Strife is a result of the interaction between the capabilities and actions of the competing sides, namely the state and the challenging group. The bargaining process between the two sides decides whether strife actually results from the interaction.

---

[1]"Conscientizing" implies the formation of a conscious sense of identity tied to a specific group and a mythology associated with that group.

STAGE 3: FROM LIKELY TO ACTUAL STRIFE

Understanding the transformation from likely to actual strife involves essentially a two-step process. The first step consists simply of investigating the nature, extent, and depth of state capabilities. This preliminary step is somewhat analogous to the previous step of establishing the requirements for successful ethnic mobilization: it completes the story about the required capabilities of the antagonists. Once state capabilities are explored, it is possible to understand the nature of feasible state responses because this latter set is bounded critically by both the nature of abstract state preferences and the state's existing capabilities. In turn, such an examination prepares the way for the second step, namely, an investigation of the nature of the strategic bargaining process. The investigation entails the matching of feasible preferences, alternative capabilities, and potential actions of both the state and the mobilized ethnic group to discover the range of possible social outcomes that could ensue from such bargaining.

In the first step—understanding state capabilities—the analyst examines the three components of state power: (1) the state's accommodative capacity, as defined by its political structure; (2) its fiscal capacity, as measured by the condition of its treasury; and (3) its coercive capacity, which refers to its ability and willingness to use effective force. When the aim is to anticipate ethnic violence, the most important variable is the state's accommodative capacity, since, as argued earlier, ethnic movements are simply a special form of political movements struggling for power. Given this fact, the most important issue for the state is its institutional structure, which is a function of two factors: the level of inclusion, as expressed by the character of the regime; and the nature of the organizational design, which enables or retards the possibility of peaceful change (or, in other words, its structured capacity for responsiveness to the demands of its constituents). The nature of the institutional structure, the prevailing norms of governance, and the cohesion of the ruling elites determine the state's accommodative capacity. Democratic, oligarchic, and authoritarian regimes vary along all three dimensions.

The fiscal capacity of the state pertains to the issue of how a state can ameliorate the demands of mobilized groups short of using force. In other words, it identifies the margins of maneuver that a state has irrespective of its political structure. Fiscal capacity has three components: (1) the overall condition of the state treasury, meaning the extent of existing surpluses and deficits and the prevailing composition of budgetary expenditures; (2) the state's potential extractive capacity, meaning the capacity to extract additional revenues without fear of accentuating political resistance; and (3) the extent and durability of its social base, meaning the size and wealth of the class supporting the ruling elites.

Coercive capacity relates, in the final analysis, to the state's ability to conclusively attempt suppression of political mobilization by force (generally the means of last resort). Its relevant components are (1) the structural relationship between the ruling elites and the instruments of violence; (2) the social composition of the military and police; (3) the state's reputation for the use of force, which incorporates historical tradition, attitudes, and experience with respect to the use of force; and (4) the technical capability of the military and police forces for suppressing unrest.

Taken together, these capabilities describe the state's latent capacity to offset popular mobilization by a group that challenges the group currently in power. They represent the state's side of the interaction with various challenging groups.

Tracking the bargaining process. Comparing the capacities of the state and the mobilized group in order to model the multidimensional process of strategic bargaining leads to an outcome that determines larger political consequences, ranging from political reconciliation to state breakdown. Some of the outcomes may result in strife of varying forms and intensity. Modeling the bargaining process entails systematically matching up the feasible preferences, alternative capabilities, and potential actions of both the mobilized ethnic group and the state to discover the range of social possibilities that such bargaining could produce. Tables and matrices presented in the next chapter (and justified theoretically in the appendix) provide the mechanistic tools for the analyst to use to model the bargaining process. The tables and matrices draw on assessments and data obtained from previous investigation.

A word of caution is in order here. The matrices and outcomes presented are emphatically not intended to be accurate "point predictions" but rather are illustrations that suggest how alternative combinations of group and state preferences and capabilities can interact to produce a variety of political consequences. Because some of these consequences embody strife in varying forms and intensity, they provide a means of "backward deduction," that is, they allow the analyst to discover which combinations of group/state preferences and capabilities are particularly volatile. If such preferences and capabilities are then seen to materialize in any given case of communal action, the intelligence analyst can "flag" such cases as potentially troublesome. These cases warrant closer scrutiny by other crisis assessment or "watch" teams, and may even justify preemptive political intervention if these strife-prone areas are of importance to the United States.

In addition, the straightforward dyadic interaction between group and state represents only one, and is in fact the simplest, kind of possible encounter. A more complex (and more realistic) situation involves not simply one ethnic group facing the state but rather several groups, possibly competing with one another *and* confronting the state simultaneously. Indeed, the role of the state can vary greatly in these situations, from that of an umpire between various contending groups to that of an abettor, if not direct precipitant, of exclusionary political action. Modeling the interactions in such a variety of settings, however, requires formal analysis that lies well beyond the scope of this preliminary effort. Consequently, the model of strategic bargaining presented here focuses on the simplest case: a dyadic encounter between a single mobilized group and the state.[2]

---

[2]The model proposed here also stems from the specific purposes of this research, namely, to capture the most important potential cases of mass violence that could lead to a U.S. military intervention. Violence between subordinate groups might be deadly and morally repulsive, but as long as the state remains "in control" it can be assumed that there would be little need for an outside intervention. But when a group challenges the state, then potential for secession and state breakdown emerges, which could then lead to an outside intervention. Since this product is designed to address a specific analytical issue with practical consequences (i.e., intervention), our scope of analysis is limited.

Modeling strategic bargaining is a three-step process, with each step forming essential building blocks for the next one. The first step involves putting together tables with which to measure the capacities of both the mobilized group and the state. The capacity of the mobilized group is measured in three areas: accommodation (its ability to be accommodative vis-à-vis the state), sustainment (its ability to sustain the political campaign for redress of its grievances), and cohesiveness (its ability to maintain the cohesiveness of its emerging group identity). Each of the three capacities is based on a combination of descriptors: leadership, access to resources and organization, and level of popular support. Variations in the mobilized group's capacity are expressed in binary terms (high/low). The capacity of the state is measured in similar (though not identical) areas: accommodation (its ability to accommodate the group's demands), sustainment (its ability to sustain its own political preferences vis-à-vis the mobilized group), and coercion (its ability to coerce the mobilized group). Each of the three capacities is based on a combination of descriptors: leadership, fiscal health of the state, and the type of regime. Variations in capacity are expressed in binary terms (high/low). Each of the eight possible combinations of descriptors for the state and the group forms one outcome (with each state and group type marked by a specific letter, ranging from A to H).

Based on the premise that each side's preferences are determined by its capacities, each of the state and group types' preference choices in the bargaining process are enumerated in two matrices (explained in detail in the next chapter and theoretically justified in the appendix). One matrix contrasts the two sets of capacity outcomes and portrays the mobilized group preferences in its cells. The other matrix contrasts the two sets of capacity outcomes and portrays the state's preferences in its cells. The range of choices is restricted to four preferences for each side. For the mobilized group, the choices are negotiation, exploitation, intimidation, and surrender. For the state, the choices are negotiation, exploitation, repression, and surrender. Repression by the state and intimidation by the group represent violent preferences. Three ranked preferences are then assigned to each outcome cell in both matrices. Resorting to violence as a first preference is the most worrisome sign in terms of anticipating strife.

The matrices conceptualize what the "political interaction" between group and state mean in terms of likely paths to conflict and strife. They form the final step in the conceptual framework for how the initial conditions of deprivation are ultimately transformed into different patterns of social strife.

Chapter Three

QUESTIONS AND GUIDELINES FOR THE ANALYST

The preceding chapter provided an outline of the model. The appendix contains a full explanation of the model, and readers interested in the detailed justification for the theoretical construct are advised to refer to that discussion. This chapter derives the practical implications of the model for the analyst through the use of questions and guidelines to address aspects of each of the three stages of the model. For the sake of clarity and to come as close as possible to specific indicators and essential elements of information, each set of questions is grouped and coded (up to four characters) with a series of letters and numbers. The coding sequence (explained below) aims to provide a step-by-step guide to organizing an analysis. The guidelines are presented so as to guide the analyst in using the tables and matrices.

The first character in the coding sequence of all questions is a capital letter (A to D) that places the question within the framework of the model. Thus, all questions pertaining to the first stage of the model—the potential for strife—start with A; all questions pertaining to the second stage of the model—the mobilization of the group for political action (thus transforming the potential into likely strife)—start with B; all questions that aim to assess the state's capabilities—the half-step of the third stage of the model that aims to establish the state's strengths and weaknesses in key areas—start with C; and all questions (really guidelines at this stage) to assess the strategic bargaining process start with D.

The second character in the coding sequence is a number that pertains to one of the subcategories in each of the three stages of the model. For all questions regarding the potential for strife (i.e., questions starting with A), the second character of the code is a number from 1 to 4 that refers either to the political factors (A1), the economic factors (A2), the social factors (A3), or the overall assessment of potential for strife (A4). For all questions on the mobilization of the group (i.e., questions starting with B), the second character of the code is a number from 1 to 6 that refers either to incipient changes (B1), galvanizing ("tipping") events (B2), leadership (B3), resources and organization (B4), the foreign element (B5), or the overall assessment of mobilization (B6). For all questions on the assessment of the state's strengths and weaknesses in key areas (i.e., questions starting with C), the second character of the code is a number from 1 to 3 that refers either to the accommodative capability (C1), the fiscal and economic capability (C2), or the coercive capability (C3). For all guidelines to assess the strategic bargaining process (i.e., questions/guidelines starting with D), the second character is a number (either 1 or 2) that is related either to the measurement of the capacities of the group and the state (D1) or the comparison of the preferences within the bargaining process (D2).

In most of the categories the breakdown continues into more specific questions or guidelines, and the codes reflect the further subcategorization. The third character is a lowercase letter (from a to e) that further distinguishes the questions and their relationship to the larger categories. For example, within the overall category of assessment of the potential for strife (A) and its subcategory of assessing closure in the political realm (A1), questions are further subdivided regarding the distribution of power among the top political executive (A1a) and security (A1b) authorities.

The coding sequence also extends in some cases to a fourth character that further differentiates some questions or guidelines within the framework of the model. The fourth character is a number from 1 to 4. For example, the subcategory explained just above (A1a) is further divided into two groups, with the code A1a1 referring to indicators that focus on the highest-ranking individuals, and A1a2 referring to the indicators of the lower-ranking bureaucrats.

A. THE POTENTIAL FOR STRIFE

Assessing the potential for strife is especially applicable to countries that lack any visible and organized ethnic movements. But the assessment is also useful for countries that do contain such movements, for it allows the analyst to ascertain the depth of the ties that bind the existing groups as well as point to the potential for new groups to arise. Both of the latter are especially useful for long-term assessment of the potential for strife.

As outlined in the model, the analysis must examine all three arenas of closure—political, economic, and social. The static "snapshot" of the current situation must be supplemented with a dynamic assessment of the ease of changing current stratification patterns. But first the analyst needs to assemble data on the substate characteristics of the given population before proceeding to the specific questions. The task involves compiling data on racial, religious, linguistic (including significant dialects), regional, or other significant cultural differences. For populations of small countries, where kinship ties may remain important, extended clan groups may also need to be examined. The purpose of the compilation is to establish the "terms of reference" for examining closure boundaries. At this point, the task is simply to note the numerical data and distribution patterns of the given subpopulation. The analyst should note discrepancies between figures for the same group provided by different sources (for a particular linguistic group, for example, members of that group and government sources may provide quite different statistics).

The outline on page 22 presents the topics of the questions that an analyst needs to consider when assessing the potential for strife. The outline is presented to make clear the organization of the section and the logical connections between the questions. The actual questions follow the outline.

A1. Assessing Closure in the Political Realm

An examination of the political realm consists of looking at the static and dynamic aspects of the distribution of power among the political executive and security authorities. Using the terms of reference already compiled (data on population characteristics), the analyst

Outline of Questions for
A. Assessing the Potential for Strife

A1. Assessing closure in the political realm
- A1a. Top political authorities
  - *A1a1. Highest-ranking individuals*
  - *A1a2. Director-level managers*
- A1b. Top security authorities
  - *A1b1. Highest-ranking individuals*
  - *A1b2. Director-level managers*
- A1c. Assessment of static factors at the political level
  - *A1c1. Comparing patterns at the political executive level*
  - *A1c2. Comparing patterns at the security level*
- A1d. Assessment of dynamic factors at the political level
  - *A1d1. General framework for change*
  - *A1d2. Framework for change by specific groups*

A2. Assessing closure in the economic realm
- A2a. Distribution of wealth
  - *A2a1. The elite level*
  - *A2a2. The general population level*
- A2b. Assessment of static factors at the economic level
- A2c. Assessment of dynamic factors at the economic level
  - *A2c1. General framework for change*
  - *A2c2. Framework for change by specific groups*

A3. Assessing closure in the social realm
- A3a. Status distribution: static aspects
  - *A3a1. Determinants of status distribution*
  - *A3a2. Benefits and restrictions based on status*
- A3b. Status distribution: dynamic aspects
  - *A3b1. General framework for change*
  - *A3b2. Framework for change by specific groups*

A4. Overall assessment of closure
- A4a. Framework for closure
  - *A4a1. Patterns of privilege and deprivation*
  - *A4a2. Degree of relative deprivation*
  - *A4a3. Potential for change*
- A4b. Ranking the groups

should examine the distribution of power among the top political executive (questions coded A1a) and security (questions coded A1b) authorities, with both the uppermost and more broadly understood upper-level officials scrutinized. The actual characteristics exhibited should then be compared with the characteristics of the population (guidelines for comparison are coded A1c). The questions and guidelines coded A1a–A1c consist of the static factors. A final element, the evaluation of dynamic factors in assessing closure in the political realm, follows (questions coded A1d). The following questions should guide the examination.

A1a. Top political authorities. The top political authorities need to be examined at two levels: the highest-ranking individuals (questions coded A1a1) and the director-level managers (questions coded A1a2) who make the everyday decisions and implement government policies. An examination of both levels is necessary so as to avoid skewed results in either area.

A1a1. Highest-ranking individuals. Which substate characteristics[1] do the top five to ten individuals in positions of executive political authority exhibit? The top executive political positions are those that carry the final responsibility for the implementation of government policy. Generally, these positions include (though may not be limited to) the president, the prime minister, and the ministers concerned with the economy (treasury, finance, industry, energy, etc.) and internal administration (interior, justice).[2] Top executive personnel in the security realm are the subject of another question (A1b1). In cases of divided government (real constraints on executive power), the legislative and/or judicial branches may also need to be examined in the manner presented above. In states where provincial administration has substantial political power (as in federal states), the key figures for the province also need to be assessed.

---

[1]The "substate characteristics" were defined a few paragraphs above at the beginning of this discussion.

[2]In some cases, the most important executive authority may not have any formal state title but instead go by "Great Leader" or "Supreme Guardian." Since the aim of the exercise is to focus on the top leaders, the analyst should go by the function performed rather than by formal title. In most cases, formal titles are the best tipoff for the function performed.

A1a2. Director-level managers. Which substate characteristics do the individuals in charge of everyday implementation of government policy exhibit? The positions in question here are sectional chiefs of the executive bureaucracy (one or two grades down from the ministerial level). The data pertain to the same ministries in the economy and security realms identified in the preceding question (A1a1). The same qualification as in A1a1 applies to states with divided governments and to states where the provinces have substantial room for independent action.

A1b. Top security authorities. The assessment of top security authorities proceeds in a fashion similar to the examination of the top political authorities, with one assessment at the level of the highest-ranking individuals (questions coded A1b1) and a complementary assessment at the director level (questions coded A1b2). The rationale for the two levels is the same as in the political-level assessment: to avoid skewed results in either area.

A1b1. Highest-ranking individuals. Which substate characteristics do the top five to ten individuals in positions of authority in the security sphere exhibit? The top positions in the security apparatus are those that carry the final responsibility for the implementation of government policy. The security apparatus consists of (but is not necessarily limited to) the following: military, police, intelligence, and foreign relations. The positions in question are the ministers and chiefs of staff for the various apparati. In states where the provincial authorities have substantial room for independent action (and have their own security structure independent of direct central control), the examination also needs to be conducted at the provincial level.

A1b2. Director-level managers. Which substate characteristics do the individuals who form the upper levels of the security apparati exhibit? The positions in question here are the upper-level ranks of the security bureaucracies identified in the preceding question (A1b1). For example, concerning the military, the ranks of the officer corps at the level of colonel and above form the group for examination. The same qualification as in A1b1 applies to states with shared central-provincial authority.

A1c. Assessment of static factors at the political level. By itself, the information assembled in A1a and A1b gives a picture of the top authorities but means little without a comparison to the conditions in the society as a whole. Any patterns that may point to closure emerge only in such a comparison. The questions below are meant to guide the comparison, with one set (coded A1c1) focusing on the political executive authorities and the other (coded A1c2) looking at the security authorities.

A1c1. Comparing patterns at the political executive level. Is there any discrepancy at the political (executive) authority level (A1a), both in terms of the elite (A1a1) and upper-level administrators (A1a2), between the actual characteristics exhibited and the characteristics of the population as a whole? Discrepancies between the actual and proportional characteristics may indicate limitations on access to power (closure). Rather than focusing on small differences, the analyst should note major differences in the two patterns (in over- and underrepresentation). For example, compare the population of country X and its political (executive) elite and top administrators in terms of linguistic preferences. Assuming that 35 percent of the country's population are native speakers of language z, the fact that 5 percent of the elite and 10 percent of the top administrators are native speakers of language z may indicate closure in the political realm (with native speakers of language z in an inferior position). In case of a comparison of the actual and proportional figures at the provincial level, the analyst should assemble data and compare both characteristics at the provincial (rather than state) level.

A1c2. Comparing patterns at the security level. What is the discrepancy in the security sphere (A1b), both in terms of the elite (A1b1) and upper-level ranks of the apparati (A1b2), between the actual characteristics exhibited and the characteristics of the population as a whole? The same guidelines outlined in A1c1 apply, in that large discrepancies (either over- or underrepresentation) between the actual and proportional characteristics may indicate limitations on access to power (closure). When provincial-level characteristics are also to be examined, the same guidelines as in A1c1 apply.

A1d. Assessment of dynamic factors at the political level. The static snapshot of possible closure that is determined in A1a–A1c needs to be supplemented by an examination of the restrictions on access to positions of power in the political and security spheres. The dynamic component is indispensable to a long-range assessment, for it provides grounds for establishing the possibility for changing the situation identified in A1a–A1c. Formal restrictions should be the primary focus (because of the ease in identifying them), but any informal restrictions also should be noted. Both the ease of change at all (questions coded A1d1) and ease of change on the part of some substate groups (questions coded A1d2) need to be examined.

A1d1. General framework for change. Is suppression of overt dissent a part of the governing process? Is there a codified process for the legitimization and/or replacement of political elites? These questions assess the overall state of development of the political institutions and establish whether a change of access to the political realm by peaceful means can realistically be contemplated.

A1d2. Framework for change by specific groups. Are there any restrictions on access to the political realm (voting rights, ability to hold office) along the lines of characteristics of the population at the substate level? Are there any restrictions at the level of substate characteristics on redress of grievances in the judicial system? Are there any restrictions on assembly along the lines of substate characteristics? Are there any restrictions on, or are any groups singled out for, service in the security apparati? Formal rules curtailing access are easily identifiable and may be found in constitutions and specific laws. Informal rules curtailing access are not as easy to identify, but in conjunction with the answers to economic (A2) and social (A3) closure indicators, they may become clear. For example, formal restrictions on access to politics may be written so as to target specific economically disadvantaged substate groups without naming those groups explicitly.

A2. Assessing Closure in the Economic Realm

Using the same terms of reference as in A1 (data on population characteristics), the analyst should examine the distribution of wealth in the society (questions coded A2a) and then compare the actual characteristics with the characteristics of the population (questions coded A2b). The resulting assessment comprises the static snapshot of the situation. Another set of questions (coded A2c) evaluates the dynamic factors in assessing closure in the economic realm. The following questions should guide the examination.

A2a. Distribution of wealth. An analysis of the distribution of wealth in a given society needs to proceed at two levels: the patterns at the elite level (questions coded A2a1) and the patterns at the level of the general population (questions coded A2a2). An examination of both levels is necessary so as to avoid skewed results in either area.

A2a1. The elite level. Which substate characteristics do the wealthiest 1 percent of the population (identified in terms of assets) exhibit? The 1 percent figure is adopted for convenience only, as a somewhat arbitrary way to identify the wealthiest; alternatively, figures anywhere from 2 to 5 percent may provide the information. The central aspect of this analysis is to identify the richest stratum of the population. Data may be difficult to obtain on this point (because of holdings in other countries), and there is an acute need for information here beyond what may be officially supplied.

A2a2. The general population level. What are the patterns of wealth (in terms of substate characteristics) in the population as a whole? A standard measure, such as per-capita income distribution, needs to be applied. The central aspect of this analysis is to identify the prevailing patterns of wealth in the population as a whole. Accurate data for this analysis may be difficult to obtain.

A2b. Assessment of static factors at the economic level. By itself, the information assembled in A2a gives a picture of the patterns of distribution of wealth, but it means little without a comparison to the breakdown of the society into substate groups according to the terms of reference gathered initially. The specific questions for the analyst are: Is there any discrepancy in the pattern of wealth distribution, both in terms of the elite (A2a1) and the general population (A2a2), between the actual characteristics exhibited and the characteristics of the population as a whole? Discrepancies between the actual and proportional characteristics may indicate limitations on access to wealth (closure). The analyst should note major differences in the patterns observed (in over- and underrepresentation). For example, compare the population of country Y and its wealthiest 1 percent and the general pattern of wealth distribution among the population in terms of religious preferences. Assume that 60 percent of the population of the country are adherents of religion x. The fact that 95 percent of the wealthiest 1 percent are adherents of religion x and that 80 percent of the wealth is concentrated in the hands of adherents of religion x may indicate closure in the economic realm.

A2c. Assessment of dynamic factors at the economic level. The static snapshot of possible closure assembled in A2a–A2b needs to be supplemented by an examination of the restrictions on access to wealth. The dynamic component is indispensable to a long-range assessment, for it provides grounds for establishing the possibility for changing the situation identified above. Formal restrictions should be the primary focus (because of the ease in identifying them), but any informal restrictions also should be noted. Both the ease of change at all (A2c1) and ease of change on the part of some substate groups (A2c2) need to be examined.

A2c1. General framework for change. Is suppression of independent economic activity a part of the governing process? Are there any fundamental noneconomic barriers to activity leading to capital accumulation? These questions assess the overall state of the economic institutions and establish whether change of access to wealth through economic means can realistically be contemplated.

A2c2. Framework for change by specific groups. Are there any restrictions on access to wealth (property laws, tax laws, limits on establishing firms) along the lines of characteristics of the population at the substate level? Are there any restrictions on consumption that may disadvantage individuals sharing certain substate characteristics? Formal rules curtailing access are easily identifiable and may be found in specific laws. Informal rules curtailing access are not as easy to identify, but in conjunction with the results of answers to political (A1) and social (A3) closure indicators, they may become clear. Formal restrictions on access to wealth may be written so as to target specific economically disadvantaged substate groups without naming those groups explicitly. Such practices might be discerned through attention to the tax structure, subsidies, trading patterns favored, and land transfer practices. For example, there might be tax preferences and/or subsidies for certain industries (and these industries might be identified with specific substate groups). In addition, certain economic activities may be defined as criminal and prosecuted. The analyst should note the informal restrictions that amount to limits on capital accumulation for some and the maintenance of wealth for those who are already wealthy.

A3. Assessing Closure in the Social Realm

Using the same terms of reference (data on population characteristics), the analyst should examine the distribution of status in the society (questions coded A3a) and the possibility for changing the pattern of status distribution (questions coded A3b). The former provides a static snapshot of the possible closure in the social realm, while the latter provides the dynamic element. Differentiation of substate groups according to status may help pinpoint some informal closure rules in the political and economic realms. The following questions should guide the examination.

A3a. Status distribution: static aspects. Because status according to substate characteristics is, by definition, accorded to the entire group, this set of questions lacks the division into two levels of analysis (elite and mass) that was necessary at the political and economic levels. Ascertaining status distribution should be carried out by looking first at the existing pattern of distribution (questions coded A3a1) and then at the specific benefits conferred or restrictions imposed on individuals belonging to a higher- or lower-status group, respectively (questions coded A3a2).

A3a1. Determinants of status distribution. What is the basis for the pattern of status hierarchy and stratification in the state (vocational, hereditary, or hierocratic)? If vocational, are there any vocations identified with specific substate groups? If hierocratic, are there any groups identified specifically with the state (is the state defined in national/group terms or not)? For example, does the constitution speak of the state as an expression of a specific national group, or does it speak of the citizens of the state (not defined in national terms)? Are there any groups seen as foreign or unassimilated? Based on status differences, the analyst should put together a status stratification map of the society, ranging from the privileged to the pariah groups.

A3a2. Benefits and restrictions based on status. What kind of benefits accrue to members of the higher-status groups simply on the basis of belonging to the group? Conversely, what kind of restraints affect members of the lower-status groups simply on the basis of belonging to the group? For example, does higher-status group membership carry exclusionary rights to participate in the political realm, or is it simply a symbolic reference that no longer carries any tangible benefits? Similarly, does belonging to a lower-status group carry any identifiable constraints on the range of economic activities in which an individual can take part? Are certain linguistic groups disadvantaged in state structures (for example, in the judiciary system)?

A3b. Status distribution: dynamic aspects. The static snapshot of possible closure that is assembled in A3a needs to be supplemented by an assessment of the rigidity of the status stratification and the extent of mobility among the status groups. The dynamic component is indispensable to a long-range assessment, for it provides grounds for establishing the possibility of changing the situation identified in A3a. Formal restrictions on membership in status groups should be the primary focus (because of the ease in identifying them), but any informal restrictions should also be noted. Both the ease of change at all (questions coded A3b1) and ease of change on the part of some substate groups (questions coded A3b2) need to be examined.

A3b1. General framework for change. How fluid is membership in a group, and is mobility between status groups possible (or are groups defined so as to preclude movement between them)? Does the state establish rules on status groups, and does it punish those who do not follow them? Is there a norm (perhaps upheld by the state) of social tolerance, or is there a norm of exclusion and separation? These questions assess the overall possibility of whether change toward belonging to a higher-status group can realistically be contemplated.

A3b2. Framework for change by specific groups. If mobility is possible, how easily is it accomplished? Are members of some groups precluded from mobility? How long might it take for an individual to change status groups? Is it a matter of rapid accomplishment in a given vocation, or is it tied to intermarriage and generations of residence in the same locality? Are certain groups especially disadvantaged by the existing rules on mobility?

A4. Overall Assessment of Closure

The examination of the specific realms of closure performed on the basis of the questions in A1–A3 has described the cleavages and potential areas of closure within the society being assessed. On the basis of the assembled information, the analyst needs to put together an assessment of the rankings of the various groups in the society. First, the analyst should establish the framework for the rankings (questions coded A4a) and then put together an explicit ranking system along the lines of discovered closure (guidelines coded A4b).

A4a. Framework for closure. The composite assessment of the framework for closure needs to make use of the information gathered so far in a manner that is most useful to the overall model. In this sense, the data gathered so far should be reinterpreted along the following lines. Using the data compiled on the characteristics of the society, which groups (if any) are privileged and which are not? (Questions coded A4a1 address this issue.) Of the groups that are not privileged, what is the degree of relative deprivation? (Questions coded A4a2 address this point.) How easy is it to change the existing inequalities and imbalances? (Questions coded A4a3 address this issue.)

A4a1. Patterns of privilege and deprivation. Do any groups show a consistent pattern of privilege or deprivation across the three realms of closure? The analyst should make the assessment on the basis of the existence of potential closure patterns established in A1c1–2, A2b, and A3a1, treating the political realm (A1c1–2) as most important. In cases where strong patterns of closure exist in all three realms, a given group may be said to be experiencing a high degree of closure (either in a position of domination or dominated). In cases of less clear-cut patterns of closure, or if the patterns do not extend across all three realms, a given group may be said to be experiencing a moderate degree of closure. If no clear pattern emerges, then closure along that specific variable may not be a factor in the given polity.

A4a2. Degree of relative deprivation. Assuming an identified high or moderate degree of closure, what is the degree of deprivation that a given group may be suffering? The analyst should make the assessment on the basis of the extent of potential closure patterns established in A1c1–2, A2b, and A3a2. Taking the most privileged group as the point of reference, how much are other groups deprived relative to it? In cases where far-reaching differences exist in all three realms, a given group may be said to be experiencing a high level of deprivation as a result of its closure. In cases where the differences are not clear-cut across the three realms, a given group may be said to be experiencing a moderate level of deprivation as a result of its closure. In cases where differences are small, then deprivation is low.

A4a3. Potential for change. Looking at the groups experiencing a high or moderate degree of closure, how amenable is the existing situation to change? The analyst should make the assessment on the basis of the dynamic factors identified in A1d, A2c, and A3b. In cases where the situation is not amenable to change at all or is amenable to change only in an extremely lengthy (generational) fashion, a given group may be said to be experiencing an extremely rigid form of closure (either in a position of domination or dominated). In cases where the situation is amenable to change in an individual's lifetime, a given group may be said to be experiencing a moderately rigid form of closure. In cases where the situation is amenable to rapid change (a matter of years), a given group may be said to be experiencing a fluid form of closure.

A4b. Ranking the groups. On the basis of the assessments in A4a, the analyst should rank order the various groups, ranging from those in a position of privilege to those that lack privilege, using the levels of deprivation and rigidity to distinguish them. The ranking represents a final assessment of the potential for certain groups to be willing to take up arms in order to change their position in the society. Rather than a strictly hierarchical ranking, some groups are likely to be advantaged in some areas and deprived in others. The analyst must take such nuances into account. The assessment represents the final results of the application of the first stage of the model to a given case.

B. TRANSFORMING POTENTIAL INTO LIKELY STRIFE

As outlined in the model, the assessments derived in the preceding section (questions coded A) point only to groups that are aggrieved and might be willing to contemplate violence in order to change the existing patterns of power and domination. In order to assess the likelihood of violence, the aggrieved groups must be analyzed in terms of mobilization potential.

There are five catalysts of mobilization that may lead to effective group action, and they need to be examined in detail. The questions below address each of the factors: incipient changes (questions coded B1), galvanizing events (questions coded B2), leadership (questions coded B3), resources and organization (questions coded B4), and the foreign element (questions coded B5). In addition, a final set of guidelines (coded B6) assesses the overall mobilization potential.

The nature of closure made a systematic examination of its components fairly straightforward; by contrast, an examination of the factors needed for mobilization lacks such a uniform structure, for two reasons. First, the time frame is different: unlike an examination of the structure and the persistent features of the society, an examination of mobilization processes has to acknowledge that mobilization can be quite rapid and surprising, even to the participants. Second, just how the five factors identified as necessary for mobilization will demonstrate themselves is exceedingly difficult to anticipate. However, thinking in terms of the five categories can shape the analyst's understanding of the mobilization and its strength, provide an early understanding that what is happening is indeed mobilization along ethnic or communitarian lines, and is crucial to understanding the third stage of the model—the bargaining process.

The outline on page 34 presents the topics of the questions that an analyst needs to consider in assessing the transformation of potential into likely strife. The outline is presented to make clear the organization of the section and the logical connections between the questions.

B1. Incipient Changes

An incipient change in closure and power relations can stem either from long-term trends (questions coded B1a) or sudden events (questions coded B1b). Ongoing small changes in a society are difficult to discern precisely because they are constant and ever present. However, long-term incremental change amounts to a fundamental change and at some point, through a specific event, the full magni-

Outline of Questions for B. Transforming Potential into Likely Strife

B1. Incipient changes
- B1a. Long-term changes
- B1b. Sudden changes

B2. Galvanizing ("tipping") events

B3. Leadership

B4. Resources and organization
- B4a. Resources
  - *B4a1. Overall availability*
  - *B4a2. Mechanisms for extraction of resources*
- B4b. Organization
- B4c. Overall assessment

B5. Foreign element
- B5a. Co-ethnics abroad
- B5b. International disputes

B6. Overall assessment of mobilization

tude of that change becomes evident in such a manner that it upsets the existing power balance. Sudden events, such as technological breakthroughs or mineral discoveries in a certain region, also threaten the existing power balance. It is possible to predict the eventual effect of long-term changes, but the changes themselves are difficult for an analyst to discern. The sudden changes are easily noted, but they are impossible to predict because they are event-specific and, by definition, unexpected. Whatever the cause, the crucial aspect here is the change in power relations and the upsetting of the status quo through a specific event.

B1a. Long-term changes. Using the terms of reference ascertained earlier, what are the demographic, economic, and environmental trends in a given society? At what point will these trends amount to pressures for systemic change? Where are such pressures most likely to materialize? For example, if two substate groups inhabit a given state and the smaller group (which is in a state of relative deprivation vis-à-vis the larger group) has double the natural growth rate of the privileged group, at some point the deprived group will become numerically larger. At that point, demands for recognition of the group's majority status (and redressing the group's deprived status) through political measures might be forthcoming. When the time is close to such a demographic shift, all the actors will understand that a change is coming. The main task for the analyst is to note the point at which long-term incremental changes amount to a basic change in power relations.

B1b. Sudden changes. Using the earlier-defined terms of reference, which groups are likely to gain and/or to lose from unexpected major breakthroughs or discoveries? For example, if major gold or oil deposits are discovered in a province that is populated primarily by a group in a subordinate position in that country, the expectation of a sudden inflow of capital into the province may amount to an unexpected shift in the power balance in the country as a whole. Unlike B1a, where the trends are possible to predict, the analyst should look at the issue of sudden changes from the perspective of monitoring ongoing events and ascertaining their impact on the larger power relations and closure in a given society. In other words, an analyst should consider specific events from the standpoint of ascertaining their potential for causing disruptions to the status quo and closure.

B2. Galvanizing ("Tipping") Events

A public event that galvanizes group sensibilities can range from the firing of an outspoken newspaper editor to a violent crackdown on the members of a given group. As such, the specific form that a galvanizing event might take is nearly impossible to predict. But through a series of questions the analyst might at least anticipate that certain events may have the potential to become galvanizing events. Keeping in mind that the central point of a galvanizing event is the symbolism behind the action, the following questions may help in narrowing the range of possibilities and should be useful in structuring the analysis. The questions focus on group anniversaries, places of special significance, prominent personalities, and group-specific cultural traits.

Are there any regularly scheduled marches or demonstrations (related, for example, to a date that holds special group-specific meaning) that may lead to a clash? Is there a specific place of symbolic significance for the group (for example, a temple or shrine) that may be subject to destruction? Is there a specific figure whose death or imprisonment will lead to his or her martyrdom? Are there any specific physical or cultural characteristics of the group (headdress, facial hair, language, certain food or drink) that may be subject to outlawing or persecution by the state? As noted above, the list is almost inexhaustible because it is event-specific, but the four distinctive categories given above provide some structure in identifying the range of choices.

B3. Leadership

Just as in the case of galvanizing events, the emergence and background of leaders is event-specific and idiosyncratic. However, as above, a skeleton analytical structure can be put together to identify likely leaders. One realm of difference is related to the type of social structures in the given society. Therefore, a basic question is whether traditional (patrimonial) or bureaucratic power structures are paramount in the society. Individuals emerging from respected organizations will be more likely to command respect and loyalty. In societies where patrimonial structures exist, some individuals assume a position of certain stature on the basis of birth and family. In societies where bureaucratic structures exist, some individuals who rise to a high position within them command a certain degree of stature. However, to be effective and act as a motivating force for the group, a leader must have a certain degree of charisma and be willing to take some risk to his safety. Keeping in mind the natural division between traditional and modern power structures that results in different types of respect and stature depending on the society, the following questions may narrow the choices in identifying potential leaders.

Are there any activists who disregard personal safety and comfort to energize the group? Are there any individuals whose speeches have a markedly and noticeably strong effect upon the audience? Are there any unusually talented individuals from a subordinate group who have risen quickly through the ranks in the armed forces or civil service? Are there leadership vehicles in place (unions, clubs, societies, etc.) so that a leader may emerge?

B4. Resources and Organization

In contrast to leadership and galvanizing events, it is easier to make an assessment of the resources (questions coded B4a) and the level of organization (questions coded B4b) of a given group. An overall composite assessment should follow (guidelines coded B4c). Since the existence of traditional (patrimonial) or modern (bureaucratic) power structures in the society affects the existence of resources and organization, the answer to that question (from answers regarding leadership issues, or B3) should be kept in mind. The following questions should assist in the analysis of the level of resources.

B4a. Resources. Resources that theoretically might be made available in conditions of full mobilization should be the goal of the assessment (questions coded B4a1), modified by an evaluation of the mechanisms for achieving full mobilization (questions coded B4a2).

B4a1. Overall availability. What are the overall levels of wealth of the group? Are there any other groups that might sympathize enough with the mobilizing group to make available some of their resources? Are there any specific wealthy individuals (either from the group or from outside of it) who sympathize with the group and/or its leader?

B4a2. Mechanisms for extraction of resources. Since the higher the deprivation the more likely a greater willingness to contribute resources, how high is the level and rigidity of deprivation of the group (also see A2b–c)? How effective a mechanism can the group construct to ensure compliance with "taxes for the group?" Does it need to rely on force for compliance, or can it rely on voluntary contributions?

B4b. Organization. The initial question on organization is whether the leader brings an existing organization to the mobilization process, for example as a result of a patrimonial basis to leadership (B3). The analyst should then attempt to assess the potential for the formation of a functioning organization on the basis of background and experiences of the group and its leader.

Does the leadership have first-hand knowledge of and experience with complex hierarchical organizations? Are there any individuals closely associated with the leader who have such knowledge or experience? What are the existing organizational mechanisms within the group that might be used by the mobilizing leader?

B4c. Overall assessment. The analyst then needs to link the answers about resources and organization (B4a–b) to assess the level of organizational effectiveness that the mobilizing group can achieve. If the leadership is in a strong position to mobilize and organize the resources of the given group, then it can be said to have high organization potential. If the leadership does not appeal to the whole group and/or is unlikely to have the organizational skills needed to utilize the resources effectively, then it can be said to have moderate organizational potential. If the leadership is weak, has limited appeal to the group as a whole, and has few of the skills needed to use the resources, then it can be said to have low organizational potential.

B5. Foreign Element

Foreign assistance is a means of boosting the mobilizing group's resource and organization base. The assistance can be distinguished along two lines: group affinity (questions coded B5a) and independent state interests (questions coded B5b).

B5a. Co-ethnics abroad. Group affinity relates to the possibility that the members of the given group inhabit areas of neighboring countries as well as form distinct diasporas as a result of immigration. The questions for the analyst focus on both types of groups. Do the state boundaries cut across a given group's homelands? Are there any identifiable irredentist organizations in the neighboring country? What kind of resources and skills can the ethnic diaspora add to the resource base of the mobilizing group? Are there identifiable mechanisms in the diaspora that can channel the resources and skills back to the group?

B5b. International disputes. Do any of the neighboring states have existing disputes with the given state? How strong are the disputes? Under what conditions might the neighboring state give support to the mobilizing group? What kind of support (in terms of resources and organization) can the neighboring state offer?

B6. Overall Assessment of Mobilization

As noted above, criteria for assessing the potential for mobilization have to remain vague because of its event-specific nature. However, the analyst should draw certain scenarios designed to elucidate the range of possibilities in resources and organization, based on (1) projection of an incipient change, (2) assumption of a galvanizing event, (3) potential emergence of three types of leader (strong, moderate, and weak), and (4) foreign support (if applicable). The drawing out of scenarios should make clear the possible consequences of mobilization. In some cases, even a strong leader might not be able to command significant resources. In other cases, even a weak leader might have substantial resources at his or her disposal. The crucial role of the leader is evident in this type of assessment of mobilization potential.

The assessment represents a way to portray the effect that an aggrieved and subordinate group might have through mobilization. Ideally, in conditions where several aggrieved groups have been identified in stage 1, the analyst should examine the mobilization potential of all of them, ranking them in terms of strength of mobilization. Just as in the final assessment in stage 1 of the model, the analyst should place the various aggrieved groups on a continuum, differentiating them by the level of mobilization potential. The differentiation represents a final assessment of the likelihood that certain groups might take up arms in order to redress their position in the society. The assessment also represents the final results of the application of the second stage of the model to a given case.

C. ASSESSING THE STATE

As outlined in the model, the mobilization of a group for political action does not necessarily lead to violence; the interaction between the state and the mobilized group may lead to any number of outcomes, ranging from peaceful reconciliation to an attempt at genocide. Anticipating what the potential outcome might be is the focus of the third stage of the model that deals with the bargaining process.

The analysis first needs to establish the state's capabilities in three categories: accommodative (questions coded C1), fiscal and economic (questions coded C2), and coercive (questions coded C3). The accommodative capability is the most important, since it pertains to the central issue of domination and monopolization of power. The results then need to be compared to the group's capabilities so as to arrive at a determination of the strategies the two actors will pursue. Establishing the state's capabilities is a step analogous to the analysis performed in stage two (questions coded B). The actual matching up of resources and elaboration of expected outcomes is a more mechanistic process, carried out with the aid of tables and matrices (guidelines coded D).

The following outline presents the topics of the questions that an analyst needs to consider in assessing the state. The outline is presented to make clear the organization of the section and the logical connections between the questions.

Outline of Questions for C. Assessing the State

C1. Accommodative capability

- C1a. Responsiveness of political structures
  - *C1a1. Level of inclusiveness*
  - *C1a2. Potential for change in political structures*
  - *C1a3. Overall assessment of responsiveness*
- C1b. Prevailing norms of governance
- C1c. Cohesion among ruling elites
- C1d. Composite assessment of accommodative capability

C2. Fiscal and economic capability

- C2a. Fiscal health
- C2b. Resource extraction potential
- C2c. Size and wealth of ruling elites
- C2d. Composite assessment of fiscal and economic capability

C3. Coercive capability

- C3a. Command and control over the apparati of violence
- C3b. Composition of the apparati of violence
- C3c. Norms toward domestic use of violence
- C3d. Suitability of the force for domestic use
- C3e. Composite assessment of coercive capability

C1. Accommodative Capability

Three categories of questions address the state's accommodative capabilities. The first category aims to ascertain the level of responsiveness of the state's political structures to popular will (questions coded C1a). The second category deals with the prevailing norms of governance that the political structures embody (questions coded C1b). The third category addresses the extent of cohesion among the ruling political elites (questions coded C1c). An overall determination of the accommodative capability is the final step (guidelines coded C1d).

C1a. Responsiveness of political structures. Assessing the responsiveness of political structures to popular will can be answered through two sets of questions. The first set addresses the level of inclusiveness of the political structures (questions coded C1a1). The second set deals with the possibility and ease of change of the political structures (questions coded C1a2). The result is a composite assessment of responsiveness (guidelines coded C1a3).

C1a1. Level of inclusiveness. Are the political structures inclusive or exclusive? Are there mechanisms in place (such as elections) that regularly hold political authorities accountable to popular will? Are there differing levels of inclusion/exclusion from the political process according to some group criteria? Are there certain groups habitually excluded from the political process on any basis, formally or informally? Constitutions and other laws are the specific indicators the analyst should consult. But the effort should go beyond the formal to the informal rules governing participation; these can be gauged from actual participation rates. The analysis should focus on evidence of low participation by a group as a potential indicator of informal exclusionary rules (some of the data gathered by the analyst while assessing closure—questions coded A—may be useful also at this stage).

C1a2. Potential for change in political structures. What are the mechanisms of conflict resolution built into the political structure? Are there established channels for change in political institutions? Again, the indicators are formal rules and laws, but whether these channels are effective needs to be assessed by discovering if changes in institutions actually occur over time. Lack of changes over a lengthy time may point to possible inflexibility of the political structures in practice even if formal rules make them appear flexible.

C1a3. Overall assessment of responsiveness. On the basis of C1a1 and C1a2, the analyst needs to assess the overall level and extent of responsiveness of the political institutions. The level of inclusiveness and the flexibility of the political structures deserve equal weight.

C1b. Prevailing norms of governance. Are there tolerant norms in place in the society, and are they reflected in state structures? The analyst should keep in mind that even if the political authorities are responsive to popular will, the state still may be prone to informal exclusion if dominant norms of intolerance are in place. The question goes beyond the formal institutional structures to the belief system underpinning them. The indicators of tolerance should be evident in the extent of effort expended in order not to exclude certain groups from participation in the political process. In certain countries, polling data on views toward other groups may be available; if reliable, such data may provide important clues as to the prevalent norms.

C1c. Cohesion among ruling elites. Is there prevailing agreement among the ruling elites about upholding the existing political structures? Are there certain elites whose actions demonstrate ambiguous views about the existing political structures? The specific indicators of cohesion should be evident from internal debates among the ruling elites. Public actions, such as obvious distancing by some of the elites, may also provide clues.

C1d. Composite assessment of accommodative capability. The assessment of the state's accommodative capability is a composite picture based on C1a–C1c, giving the most importance to factors of responsiveness (C1a), determined in C1a3. Democratic states are bound to score better than authoritarian ones in responsiveness. However, responsiveness may vary considerably among democratic states. States with new democratic structures may be quite different in their level of responsiveness from long-standing states where inclusionary institutions have had a chance to develop and norms of tolerance have been internalized. In this sense, C1b can be an important modifier of the assessment arrived at in C1a3. In addition, the presence of factions in the ruling elite that have doubts about upholding the existing political structures lowers the accommodative capability of the state even if the assessments in C1a and C1b may give the state an otherwise high mark in this category.

C2. Fiscal and Economic Capability

Three sets of questions address the issue of economic resources that the state can amass in its competition with the mobilized group. The category is important because it establishes the bounds on how well the state can deal with the group and its demands without resorting to force. The first set of questions deals with the state's overall fiscal health (questions coded C2a). These questions address the financial resources readily available to the state. The second set of questions pertains to the resources that potentially could be extracted from the society by the state machinery and made available for the competition with the mobilized group (questions coded C2b). The third set of questions deals with the size and wealth of the main group that is represented by the ruling elites (questions coded C2c). On the basis of the assessments in each category, an overall assessment of the state's fiscal and economic capabilities needs to be made (guidelines coded C2d).

C2a. Fiscal health. Is the state engaged in deficit spending, or is it amassing surpluses? If it is deficit spending, has the trend gone on for some time? What is the burden imposed on the state treasury by payment of debt and interest? How is the budget appropriated, and could the state make substantial shifts in how the funds are appropriated? For example, could substantial funds be transferred from defense to specifically targeted social spending? Data to determine the health of the treasury are generally available from official sources, though they should be assessed first for reliability.

C2b. Resource extraction potential. How much slack is there in terms of the state being able to increase the rate of extraction of resources from the society? Is the tax burden at such a high level that a significant increase will be counterproductive (flight of capital, substantial erosion of political support)? Or are tax burdens fairly low and are there readily identifiable areas of wealth? And is the bureaucratic machinery in place able to collect the additional resources? Some of the data to answer these questions should be readily available in official publications. The comparative assessment of whether the tax burden is low or high needs to be made on the basis of real tax rates per capita and investment climate (as rated by international banks) against countries at similar development levels (potential competitors for foreign investment). An evaluation of the efficiency of the tax collection bureaucracy (based on indicators such as estimates of levels of tax evasion) also needs to be made.

C2c. Size and wealth of ruling elites. What is the size and level of wealth of the ruling elite's core constituency (the group whose interests the ruling elite represents the most)? What are the comparative wealth levels of this group vis-à-vis the population as a whole? How high of a real tax burden (with taxes understood in the wide meaning of the term) is the group facing at this time? And what are the levels of tax burden that the core group might be willing to endure in order to support the ruling elite? In other words, is it likely that the main social base for the ruling elite will be willing to endure higher burdens than the general population in order to keep its privileged position? Data to answer these questions stem more likely than not from estimates derived from general tax burden levels.

C2d. Composite assessment of fiscal and economic capability. The assessment of the fiscal and economic capability of the state is based on a composite of C2a–C2c, so as to incorporate both the present and the potential level of mobilization of resources by the state. All three factors play a major role, and strength in one area can offset weaknesses in another.

C3. Coercive Capability

Four separate sets of questions address the ability of the state to marshal and use force in its competition with the mobilized group. First, what are the structural command-and-control links between the ruling elites and the apparati of violence, such as the police, militia, and the armed forces (questions coded C3a)? This is the most important of the four factors. Second, what is the composition—at the rank-and-file level—of these apparati (questions coded C3b)? Third, what are the norms toward and experience with respect to the use of force against internal opponents (questions coded C3c)? Fourth, how capable are the apparati of violence in dealing with internal opposition (questions coded C3d)? A final assessment of the coercive capability is based on an examination of all of these factors (guidelines coded C3e).

C3a. Command and control over the apparati of violence. What are the mechanisms for ordering the use of the police and/or the military against internal opponents? Is the process subject to influence and opinions of others than just the top executive authority? Do any other political structures—besides the executive—affect the extent of employment of the apparati of violence against domestic opponents? The indicators of the structural constraints (or lack thereof) on executive authority and command of internal use of the apparati of violence are embedded in the legal rules governing the use of force. An evaluation of how closely such rules are followed in practice is an essential component of the assessment.

C3b. Composition of the apparati of violence. Who serves in the apparati of violence? Are some groups overrepresented? Is the rank and file likely to follow the orders of the top authorities? How likely is the rank and file to identify with an aggrieved group? The data on the composition of the police and the military may be sensitive, especially in states where internal problems are severe. Intelligence sources may be needed to supplement data from open sources. The assessment should focus on the units most likely to be used for internal purposes, though data for all of the police and the military should be taken into account.

C3c. Norms toward domestic use of violence. What is the state's propensity for the use of force, based on historical tradition and experiences? Does the state have a long-standing reputation for relying on the apparati of violence to quell internal dissent? Have the apparati of violence been used for such purposes within the past two to three decades (one generation)? The data for this assessment are openly available and based on the historical record.

C3d. Suitability of the force for domestic use. Is the equipment and training of the apparati of violence suitable for quelling internal unrest? Are there units (in either the police or the military) that have a specific internal orientation (such as anti-riot units)? How large are such forces? The data for this assessment should be openly available, though some details (equipment of the anti-riot police) may be more difficult to locate. Evaluations of the training of domestically tasked units by outside observers also would be helpful in assessing the proficiency of such formations.

C3e. Composite assessment of coercive capability. The assessment of the coercive capability of the state is based on a composite of C3a–C3d, with particular attention to C3a (because of its crucial role in constraining the decisionmaking process regarding the use of force).

D. STRATEGIC BARGAINING

The bargaining process between a mobilized group and the state determines whether the outcome of the process will be violence, peaceful reconciliation, or some point in between. Both the group's and the state's preferences are structured by their own strengths and weaknesses as well as the opponent's strengths and weaknesses. The optimal strategy is one based on maximum cost-effectiveness (in political terms). In other words, the strategies the group and the state will pursue stem from the specific characteristics of each relative to the opponent. Rather than questions for the analyst, this section consists of guidelines, for the task here is to model the interaction on the basis of the data gathered so far.

Modeling the interactive process to anticipate the potential for violence requires placing the information gathered so far on the group and the state into a format that categorizes each into a specific state or group type. Using two tables that describe the state and group capacities (guidelines for measuring the capacities are coded D1), the analyst creates a composite picture of the essential strengths and weaknesses of the group and the state. The interaction between each type of group and each type of state is then simulated with the help of two matrices (guidelines on using the matrices are coded D2). A comparison of the preferences of the state and the group illustrates a likely outcome. Whether the outcome is violent or not addresses the fundamental point of the entire exercise—that is, the likelihood of violence.

The following outline presents the organization of the guidelines and the logical connections between the steps that an analyst needs to perform to come up with a final assessment on the likelihood of strife that might result from the bargaining process.

Outline of Guidelines for D. Strategic Bargaining

D1. Measuring the Capacities of the Group and the State

The first step is to measure the capacities of the group (guidelines coded D1a) and the state (guidelines coded D1b) in three critical areas. The critical areas are similar, though not the same, for the state and the group. The data for the measurement are based on assessments from previous sections (coded B and C). The measurements categorize the group and the state into one of eight specific types. The eight types comprise all of the possible combinations of the three categories, each coded in a binary fashion. The analyst must make some difficult choices at this point. The gathered data can structure the decision, but there is no way to avoid subjective reasoning in making an assessment based on only two choices.

D1a. Measuring the group's capacities. Categorizing the group in terms of three essential capacities—accommodative, sustainment, and cohesiveness—requires a binary assessment of leadership, resources, and the level of popular support of the group. Accommodative capacity measures the group's ability to accommodate its goals to the other competing social formations, especially the state. Sustainment capacity measures the group's ability to sustain its political campaign as it attempts to redress its grievances. Cohesiveness measures the group's ability to maintain group identity in the process of pursuing its aims. The manner and strength of the group's mobilization determines its capacity in each of the three critical categories. Arriving at the determination means ranking the group in three areas: leadership (guidelines coded D1a1), sustainment (guidelines coded D1a2), and cohesiveness (guidelines coded D1a3). The specific rankings then determine the group type (guidelines coded D1a4).

D1a1. Group capacity: leadership. The analyst must rate the group in terms of leadership: strong or weak. Strong leadership is defined as having the following characteristics: (1) self-confident and secure in its position, (2) willing to take some risks of losing popularity in order to achieve its ends, and (3) owning a clear view of the goals it wants to accomplish. Weak leadership is defined as having the following characteristics: (1) conscious of other potential leaders, (2) unable to afford to take risks and obliged to appeal to the group broadly, even if such action compromises the goals, and (3) liable to waver in dedication to the goals. The assessments derived in the section on group mobilization regarding leadership (questions coded B3) should form the building block for a rating of the leadership.

D1a2. Group capacity: sustainment. The analyst must rate the group in terms of resource support: good or weak. Good resource support is defined as (1) sufficient support to meet all near-term objectives, most mid-term objectives, and some long-term objectives, (2) real prospects of increased support as the group gains momentum, and (3) available support that is suited to means and ends. Weak resource support is defined as (1) insufficient support to meet even all near-term objectives, causing expenditure of considerable efforts to obtain support, perhaps even driving the group into survival mode, (2) limited or uncertain prospects of increased support, and (3) a mismatch between available support and means and ends. The assessments derived in the section on group mobilization regarding resources and organization (questions coded B4) as well as foreign support (questions coded B5) should form the building block for a rating of resource support.

D1a3. Group capacity: cohesiveness. The analyst must rate the group in terms of popular support: broad or weak. Broad popular support is defined as (1) strong appeal of the leadership's ideas to the group and (2) potential for sympathy and/or support from other groups. Weak popular support is defined as (1) weak resonance of the ideas beyond the leadership (ideas are either not fully or not widely accepted) and (2) no potential for support from other groups. The assessments derived in the section on group mobilization regarding incipient changes (questions coded B1), galvanizing events (questions coded B2), and the overall strength of mobilization and group identity (questions coded B6) should form the building block for a rating of popular support.

D1a4. Locating the group type. Based on a rating in each of the three categories above, the analyst should locate the group type for the specific group being examined. Each type of group (one of eight types, ranging from A to H), has corresponding capacities in the three critical areas (see Table 3.1).

D1b. Measuring the state's capacities. Categorizing the state in terms of three essential capacities—accommodative, sustainment, and coercive—requires a binary assessment of leadership, the fiscal health of the state, and the regime type. Accommodative capacity measures the state's ability to accommodate the group's demands. Sustainment capacity measures the state's ability to sustain its political preferences in competition with the group. Coercive capacity measures the state's ability to coerce the opponents into compliance. The political structure of the state, the state's potential for the use of force, and its fiscal and economic health determine its capacity in each of the three critical categories. Arriving at the determination means ranking the state in three areas: leadership (guidelines coded D1b1), fiscal health (guidelines coded D1b2), and regime type (guidelines coded D1b3). The specific rankings then determine the state type (guidelines coded D1b4).

D1b1. State capacity: leadership. The analyst must rate the state in terms of leadership: strong or weak. Strong leadership is defined in the same manner as for the group, and it has the following characteristics: (1) self-confident and secure in its position, (2) willing to risk losing popularity in order to achieve its ends, and (3) owning a clear view of the goals it wants to accomplish. Weak leadership is also defined in the same manner as the group, and it has the following characteristics: (1) conscious of other potential leaders, (2) unable to afford to take risks and obliged to appeal to the group broadly, even if such action compromises the goals, and (3) liable to waver in dedication to the goals. The assessments derived in the section regarding the political structure (questions coded C1) are the shaping influ-

Table 3.1

Capacity of a Mobilized Group

Type of Mobilized Group		Capacity		
Code	Descriptors	Accommodative	Sustainment	Cohesiveness
A	Strong leadership Good resource support Broad popular support	High	High	High
B	Weak leadership Good resource support Broad popular support	Low	High	Low
C	Strong leadership Weak resource support Broad popular support	High	Low	High
D	Strong leadership Good resource support Weak popular support	Low	High	High
E	Weak leadership Weak resource support Broad popular support	Low	Low	Low
F	Weak leadership Weak resource support Weak popular support	High	Low	Low
G	Strong leadership Weak resource support Weak popular support	Low	Low	Low
H	Weak leadership Good resource support Weak popular support	Low	High	Low

ences on any specific leadership in power. The structural elements are more important than the specific personalities in question, though some knowledge of the current leadership is also necessary.

D1b2. State capacity: fiscal position. The analyst must rate the state in terms of its fiscal position: strong or weak. Strong fiscal position is defined as having the following characteristics: (1) budget surpluses or low deficits, (2) room for major reallocations within the structure of the budget, (3) enough wealth for increased revenue generation. Weak fiscal position is defined as having the following characteristics: (1) deep and/or prolonged deficit spending, (2) highly constrained room for reallocation within the budget, and (3) limited potential for increased revenue generation due to limited wealth. The assessments derived in the section regarding the fiscal and economic health of the state (questions coded C2) should form the building block for a rating of the fiscal position.

D1b3. State capacity: regime type. The analyst must rate the state by regime type: inclusive or exclusive. Although the two choices have some overlap with democratic and nondemocratic regime types, the terms are not the same, for they focus on both the normative and the institutional aspects. An inclusive regime is defined as having the following characteristics: (1) competitive elections and unrestricted rights to assembly, (2) uncensored media, (3) limits on the executive power, and (4) prevailing norms of tolerance. An exclusive regime is defined as having the following characteristics: (1) lack of competitive elections and/or restrictions on rights to assembly, (2) restrictions on or censorship of the media, (3) no real check on the executive power, and (4) weak or nonexistent norms of tolerance. Almost all democratic regimes are inclusive, but not all inclusive regimes are democratic. Similarly, almost all oligarchic or authoritarian regimes are exclusive, but not all exclusive regimes are nondemocratic. The assessments regarding political structure (questions coded C1) and the apparati of coercion (questions coded C3) should form the building blocks for rating a state on regime type.

D1b4. Locating the state type. Based on a rating in each of the three categories above, the analyst can locate the state type for the specific state being examined. Each type of state (one of eight types, ranging from A to H) has corresponding capacities in the three critical areas (see Table 3.2).

Table 3.2

Capacity of the State

Type of State		Capacity		
Code	Descriptors	Accommodative	Sustainment	Coercive
A	Strong leadership Strong fiscal position Inclusive regime	High	High	Low
B	Weak leadership Strong fiscal position Inclusive regime	Low	Low	High
C	Strong leadership Weak fiscal position Inclusive regime	High	Low	Low
D	Strong leadership Strong fiscal position Exclusive regime	Low	Low	High
E	Weak leadership Weak fiscal position Inclusive regime	High	Low	Low
F	Weak leadership Weak fiscal position Exclusive regime	Low	Low	Low
G	Strong leadership Weak fiscal position Exclusive regime	Low	Low	High
H	Weak leadership Strong fiscal position Exclusive regime	Low	High	High

D2. Comparing Preferences Within the Bargaining Process

Once the analyst has defined the group and the state as fitting one particular state and group type, the next step is to locate the specific preferences of each on a matrix of preference choices. This is essentially a mechanical step, carried out in two stages: figuring out the preferences of the group toward the state (guidelines coded D2a) and figuring out the preferences of the state toward the group (guidelines coded D2b). The interaction of the two preferences makes up the final assessment of whether violence is likely (guidelines coded D2c).

D2a. Preferences of the group toward the state. Using Matrix 3.1, the analyst locates the column appropriate to the specific type of state that the group is facing. For example, if the specific determination from D1 has concluded that the situation pits group type D against a state type C, the analyst would locate group D at the left of the matrix and, using the row of group type D, look at the set of three preferences in the column under state type C. Circling the specific three preferences in the matrix, the choices are (1) Neg, (2) Exp, and (3) Int. (An explanation of the preferences follows in D2c.)

D2b. Preferences of the state toward the group. Using Matrix 3.2, the analyst should locate the row appropriate to the specific type of group that the state is facing. As in the example used in D2a, if the specific determination from D1 has concluded that the situation pits state type C against a group type D, the analyst would locate state type C at the top of the matrix and, using the row for group type D, look at the set of three preferences in the column under state type C. Circling the specific three preferences in the matrix, the choices are (1) Rep, (2) Exp, and (3) Neg. (An explanation of the preferences follows in D2c.)

D2c. Final outcome: preferences for violence. Combining D2a and D2b determines the likelihood of violence in the given case. There are four preference choices used in each matrix. For the state, the preferences are "Rep" (repress), meaning the use of violence against the group; "Exp" (exploit), meaning the use of nonviolent means to compete with the group; "Neg" (negotiate), meaning the use of peaceful negotiation; and "Sur" (surrender), meaning the state surrenders to the demands of the group. For the group, the preferences are "Int" (intimidate), meaning the use of violence against the state; "Exp" (exploit), meaning the use of nonviolent means to compete with the state; "Neg" (negotiate), meaning the use of peaceful negotiation; and "Sur" (surrender), meaning the group surrenders to the pressure by the state.

The three preferences comprise the likely strategies to be followed by the state and the group against a specific opponent. The choices

Matrix 3.1

Mobilized Group Preferences

Mobilized Group Type	State Type (Table 3.2)							
(Table 3.1)	A	B	C	D	E	F	G	H
A	1. Neg 2. Exp 3. Int	1. Exp 2. Int 3. Neg	1. Neg 2. Exp 3. Int	1. Int 2. Exp 3. Neg	1. Neg 2. Exp 3. Int	1. Exp 2. Int 3. Neg	1. Int 2. Exp 3. Neg	1. Exp 2. Int 3. Neg
B	1. Exp 2. Int 3. Neg	1. Int 2. Exp 3. Neg	1. Neg 2. Exp 3. Int	1. Int 2. Neg 3. Int	1. Int 2. Exp 3. Neg	1. Int 2. Exp 3. Neg	1. Exp 2. Neg 3. Int	1. Exp 2. Int 3. Neg
C	1. Neg 2. Exp 3. Int	1. Exp 2. Neg 3. Int	1. Neg 2. Exp 3. Int	1. Int 2. Neg 3. Exp	1. Exp 2. Int 3. Neg	1. Int 2. Exp 3. Neg	1. Int 2. Exp 3. Neg	1. Exp 2. Int 3. Neg
D	1. Neg 2. Exp 3. Int	1. Exp 2. Neg 3. Int	1. Neg 2. Exp 3. Int	1. Int 2. Exp 3. Neg	1. Int 2. Exp 3. Int	1. Int 2. Exp 3. Neg	1. Exp 2. Neg 3. Int	1. Exp 2. Neg 3. Int
E	1. Exp 2. Neg 3. Int	1. Exp 2. Int 3. Neg	1. Exp 2. Neg 3. Int	1. Exp 2. Neg 3. Int	1. Exp 2. Int 3. Neg	1. Int 2. Exp 3. Neg	1. Neg 2. Exp 3. Sur	1. Exp 2. Int 3. Neg
F	1. Neg 2. Exp 3. Sur	1. Exp 2. Neg 3. Sur	1. Neg 2. Exp 3. Int	1. Neg 2. Exp 3. Sur	1. Exp 2. Int 3. Neg	1. Exp 2. Int 3. Neg	1. Exp 2. Neg 3. Sur	1. Exp 2. Int 3. Neg
G	1. Exp 2. Neg 3. Int	1. Int 2. Exp 3. Neg	1. Neg 2. Exp 3. Int	1. Int 2. Neg 3. Exp	1. Int 2. Exp 3. Neg	1. Int 2. Exp 3. Neg	1. Exp 2. Int 3. Neg	1. Int 2. Exp 3. Neg
H	1. Exp 2. Neg 3. Sur	1. Exp 2. Int 3. Neg	1. Exp 2. Int 3. Neg	1. Exp 2. Int 3. Neg	1. Int 2. Exp 3. Neg	1. Int 2. Exp 3. Neg	1. Exp 2. Int 3. Neg	1. Exp 2. Neg 3. Int

Matrix 3.2

State Preferences

Mobilized Group Type (Table 3.1)	State Type (Table 3.2)							
	A	B	C	D	E	F	G	H
A	1. Neg 2. Exp 3. Rep	1. Neg 2. Exp 3. Rep	1. Neg 2. Exp 3. Rep	1. Rep 2. Neg 3. Rep	1. Neg 2. Exp 3. Sur	1. Rep 2. Exp 3. Neg	1. Rep 2. Exp 3. Neg	1. Exp 2. Rep 3. Neg
B	1. Exp 2. Neg 3. Rep	1. Neg 2. Exp 3. Rep	1. Neg 2. Exp 3. Rep	1. Exp 2. Rep 3. Neg	1. Neg 2. Exp 3. Rep	1. Exp 2. Rep 3. Neg	1. Exp 2. Neg 3. Rep	1. Exp 2. Rep 3. Neg
C	1. Neg 2. Exp 3. Rep	1. Neg 2. Exp 3. Rep	1. Neg 2. Exp 3. Rep	1. Rep 2. Exp 3. Neg	1. Neg 2. Exp 3. Sur	1. Rep 2. Exp 3. Neg	1. Rep 2. Exp 3. Neg	1. Rep 2. Exp 3. Neg
D	1. Rep 2. Neg 3. Exp	1. Neg 2. Rep 3. Exp	1. Rep 2. Exp 3. Neg	1. Rep 2. Exp 3. Neg	1. Neg 2. Exp 3. Rep	1. Rep 2. Exp 3. Neg	1. Rep 2. Exp 3. Neg	1. Rep 2. Exp 3. Neg
E	1. Exp 2. Neg 3. Rep	1. Neg 2. Exp 3. Rep	1. Exp 2. Neg 3. Rep	1. Exp 2. Neg 3. Rep	1. Neg 2. Exp 3. Rep	1. Rep 2. Exp 3. Neg	1. Exp 2. Neg 3. Rep	1. Rep 2. Exp 3. Neg
F	1. Rep 2. Exp 3. Neg	1. Neg 2. Exp 3. Rep	1. Rep 2. Exp 3. Neg	1. Rep 2. Exp 3. Neg	1. Neg 2. Rep 3. Exp	1. Exp 2. Rep 3. Neg	1. Rep 2. Exp 3. Neg	1. Rep 2. Exp 3. Neg
G	1. Rep 2. Neg 3. Exp	1. Neg 2. Exp 3. Rep	1. Rep 2. Exp 3. Neg	1. Rep 2. Exp 3. Neg	1. Neg 2. Exp 3. Rep	1. Rep 2. Exp 3. Neg	1. Rep 2. Exp 3. Neg	1. Exp 2. Rep 3. Neg
H	1. Rep 2. Exp 3. Neg	1. Neg 2. Exp 3. Rep	1. Rep 2. Exp 3. Neg	1. Rep 2. Exp 3. Neg	1. Neg 2. Exp 3. Rep	1. Exp 2. Rep 3. Neg	1. Rep 2. Exp 3. Neg	1. Exp 2. Rep 3. Neg

stem from the specific arrangement of two sides' strengths and weaknesses. The first preference is the primary strategy that either the group or the state is likely to follow. The second preference is the alternative strategy that the group or state may follow. The third choice provides another option that the state or group may consider. The three choices presented here are analytical constructs; in practice the real strategies are likely to be a mixture of the top two or even all three choices, though the top choice generally will be the dominant strategy. For example, if the choices for a state come up as "Negotiate, Repress, Exploit" (in that order) in practice, the strategy of such a state might consist of a sincere negotiating attempt, simultaneously keeping ready a strong capability to crack down on the group (and a readiness to use force, if necessary), and occasional attempts to embarrass or reduce the standing of the group through selective economic or media actions.

Although the preferences do not necessarily imply a temporal dimension, the second strategic preference should be considered by the analyst as having the potential of being followed if the primary strategy is not adopted or is not bearing the desired result. The third preference is included to complete the theoretical picture, but it is likely to be a hedging strategy at best.

Because the final result is always an interaction of the two sides' preferences, a first preference for violence by either the state or the group should be flagged by the analyst as an indication that strife is likely. In cases where both first preferences are for a violent outcome, the potential for violence (perhaps even a very severe type of violence) is high. In cases where neither of the first preferences are for violence, the analyst should look at the second preferences. If one of them is for violence, the case may require monitoring.

A word of caution is in order on using the matrices. Results indicating violent outcomes should not be taken as empirical, for they are not. Instead, the results are theoretically justified likely outcomes based on the structure presented above. That is why it is not advisable for the analyst to limit his or her judgment only to first preferences.

The suggested format for the analyst is to treat any first preference that includes violence as a "red marker" (violence is likely), any second preference for violence as a "yellow marker" (violence possible but could be averted), and any third preference for violence as a "green marker" (violence unlikely).

FINAL OBSERVATIONS ON USING THE HANDBOOK

The specific utility of the model proposed here and explained step by step in the handbook is to structure the analysis. Indeed, the value of the process outlined here is that it can be delineated at each step, and the specific rationale for anticipating violence can be explained. This is the advantage and the contribution of the model and the methodology outlined above. However, as should be abundantly clear by now, the model structures the analyst's work but does not eliminate the need for his or her informed but subjective judgments throughout the process explained above.

Through the use of specific scenarios, even hypothetical situations (centering on different types of group mobilization) can be modeled with the use of the framework given above. For example, in cases where ethnic groups are not mobilized, the analyst can determine (on the basis of conditions derived in the section on the potential for violence, or questions coded A) the possibility of mobilization along ethnic lines, the potential pathways of mobilization, and their likely consequences. Such an exercise has a specific long-term warning use.

Similarly, through the use of scenarios, the unfolding of group mobilization may be modeled even though all of the elements of mobilization might not yet be in place. Such modeling can point to potential paths that, if identified early, may lead to warning and preparation.

Although, as noted earlier, the model is not designed for analysis of multigroup situations, some analysts may use it to think about the dynamics in situations that are more complex than the simple dyadic interaction presented above. To model such cases, the analyst should group the potential challengers to the state into one "supergroup." If tensions among the components of such a supergroup are likely, then coding of the leadership and popular support aspects of the group will be affected. For heuristic purposes, the use of the model in such a manner may suffice, but it is not a perfect tool by any means to deal with the more complex situations.

Appendix

THE THEORETICAL MODEL

This appendix provides the theoretical model that underpins the framework presented in the handbook. The model was developed to help the Army in particular and the intelligence community in general anticipate the rise of ethnic tension long before it manifests itself in actual violence.[1] Toward this end, the model provides a conceptual overview of the processes triggering political mobilization along ethnic lines as well as a framework for understanding state responses, both of which interact to produce either political reconciliation leading to peace or political breakdown resulting in violence. This model draws on the insights of social science (especially political science, economics, and sociology) from the past several decades, especially as developed in the subfields of rational-choice theory, ethnicity and nationalism, and collective violence, in order to understand the phenomenon of ethnic challenges to state power.

There are three important considerations to be borne in mind when scrutinizing this model.

First, the model is intended primarily to help the intelligence community *order its thinking* about the logic and dynamics of potential ethnic violence, and to systematically organize the *information-collection requirements* relating to the problem. Understanding this intention is critical to appraising the adequacy of the effort. Most of

[1]The term "model" is used throughout this appendix in the conventional sense familiar to the social sciences. It represents a closed system of causal statements providing a theoretical explanation of the phenomenon—ethnic violence—under consideration. For an analysis of the concept of a theoretical model, see Max Black, *Models and Metaphors*, Ithaca: Cornell University Press, 1962.

the aids now used by the intelligence community are large-scale inductive models that statistically "grind up" enormous amounts of data—ranging from health and mortality statistics to the number of individuals under arms—to try to develop useful predictors of political violence. Such predictors, if at all finally available, merely describe a correlation between some class of data and political violence; they do not establish a *causal* link between the variables included and the social outcome they seek to explain. Not surprisingly, such inductive models cannot ask the right questions that bear on the problem of how deprivation and discontent lead to strife. Consequently, they cannot generate a targeted set of information requirements for intelligence agencies to pursue and thereby increase understanding and predictability with respect to the problem of ethnic violence.

Second, this model is intended to provide a *general conceptual framework* that speaks to the issue of how ethnic mobilization occurs and how it could lead to violence under certain conditions. It incorporates the insights offered by various theories that focus on separate aspects of the problem—such as, for example, the relative deprivation of the populace or the extent of state capacity—into a more comprehensive structure that encompasses the entire *process* of ethnic mobilization from the roots of conflict all the way to social reconciliation or state breakdown. Having said this, however, it is important to recognize that this framework does not proffer any specific "theory" of ethnic conflict, understood as explaining "why" ethnic conflicts occur in some "ultimate" sense. Rather, the framework offered here is fundamentally an "analog" model in the sense that it aims to identify what, if any, step-level disturbances must occur before the prevailing political system is transformed from one formal operating state into another.

This objective is particularly appropriate for purposes of "indication and warning," where the focus is not so much to divine why ethnic conflicts arise in some "essentialist" way but rather to identify which critical variables are relevant for anticipating its outbreak and what might happen if some of these variables disturb some other variables in the explanatory system. While this task no doubt requires some implicit understanding of the causal drivers of conflict, the emphasis nonetheless is *not* on explicating the various causes and patterns of ethnic conflict per se but instead on developing a "model" that reproduces the structure and relationships within the process of ethnic mobilization in an eidetically adequate way.[2]

Third, this model is focused primarily on helping the intelligence community with the problem of *long-range assessment of possible ethnic strife* rather than with forecasting imminent ethnic violence and state breakdown. While the model speaks to some of these latter issues, it lacks the level of detail required to provide adequate predictions of such violence under a variety of conditions. Incorporating such detail would require more "intensive" sorts of explanations and would be very useful for intelligence analysts tasked with monitoring day-to-day flows of events. However, such models would by definition presume that ethnically driven competition is already under way and, hence, would be less useful from the perspective of trying to assess when and under what conditions ethnic mobilization may in fact come about (just the kind of work that forms the staple of analyses focusing on various long-range futures facing a given state or region). It is also important to recognize that for a variety of theoretical reasons it is probably impossible to develop any *single* model that can explain imminent ethnic breakdown. Instead, multiple models would probably be required, and these models would vary based on the outcomes sought to be explained (that is, mass refugee movements, ethnic violence, genocide, and state collapse, for example, would each require separate models) as well as on the relative weights assigned to various remote causes, proximate causes, and event sequences that combine to produce such outcomes. There are already several such efforts under way in the academic community. Replicating them is not only uneconomical, it does not serve the analyst focusing on long-range assessment, who is the primary consumer of this research.

It is also worth mentioning that while the model is intended to provide a general framework for understanding the key structural factors that could lead under certain conditions to ethnic strife, it is *not* designed as a computational device that "automatically" produces predictions of ethnic violence given suitable information. It is in

---

[2]This is precisely the meaning of an "analog" model as opposed to a "theoretical" model. For further detail about the differences between the two structures of scientific explanation, see Max Black, *Models and Metaphors*, Ithaca: Cornell University Press, 1962, p. 223.

fact—emphatically—not intended to be a mechanistic substitute for knowledge, reasoning, or judgment on the part of regional intelligence analysts but "merely" a means of helping them order the information already at their command (and identifying needed but missing information) as they attempt to assess the prospects for ethnic breakdown in any given region or part of the world.

A basic assumption of this analysis, of course, is that human behavior, both individually and in collectivities, is rational and can be understood. The assumption goes against some popular beliefs about ethnic conflict as irrational. Such beliefs are often less explanations than despairing reactions to a difficult phenomenon. If human behavior is irrational, then it cannot be predicted or even anticipated. If, on the other hand, communal and particularly ethnic strife fits into the more general category of social and political competition, its dynamics may be understandable, so a more effective anticipation of such conflicts may indeed be possible.

This appendix consists of two principal sections followed by a conclusion. The first section elaborates the main approaches to ethnicity—the primordial, the epiphenomenal, and the ascriptive—pervading the literature. Much confusion has resulted from imprecise or different definitions of "ethnicity." This section makes the assumptions explicit and presents the framework on which the theoretical model builds.

Developing out of the ascriptive tradition, the subsequent section explicates the theoretical model designed to help the intelligence community anticipate the outbreak of ethnically based forms of strife. It explains how the potential for strife should be understood; how the potential for strife is transformed, through mobilization, into a likelihood of strife; and how extant state capacities interact through a process of strategic bargaining with mobilized groups to produce, under certain conditions, varying degrees of strife.

The concluding section of the appendix briefly identifies the limitations of this analysis and indicates the tasks for future research.

Approaches to Ethnicity

DEFINITIONAL PROBLEMS

The definition of ethnicity remains one of the most contested categories in social science. Due in part to the definitional problem, the relationship between ethnicity and other classificatory categories such as race, nation, and class remains poorly understood. In fact, the pioneer of modern sociology, Max Weber, even while producing one of the most sophisticated social scientific frameworks that could be applied to analyze ethnicity, concluded that

> the notion of "ethnically" determined social action subsumes phenomena that a rigorous sociological analysis . . . would have to distinguish carefully . . . [and] . . . it is certain that in this process the collective term "ethnic" would be abandoned, for it is unsuitable for a really rigorous analysis."[3]

Considerable scholarly attention to the phenomenon over the past three decades seemingly has been intent on proving Weber wrong. The more recent analyses of ethnicity have taken a variety of approaches and produced some sophisticated new insights. But when these disparate approaches are analyzed systematically, they usually fall into one of three main "ideal types" relating to ethnicity as a social phenomenon, each with a distinctive perspective on what ethnicity is and how it relates to social conflict.

These three approaches are discussed below. The principal insights are first systematically described, followed by the particular explanation of the linkages between ethnicity and group conflict. The strengths and weaknesses of each approach are then analyzed with respect to group solidarity and collective action. "Group solidarity" refers to the existence of deep bonds between members of a particular social grouping. "Collective action" refers to the basic problem facing any group action, namely, the fact that contributing to collective action may not be rational for an individual and, as such, may result in the failure of group efforts.

---

[3]Max Weber, *Economy and Society*, Vol. 1, Guenter Roth and Claus Wittich (eds.), Berkeley: University of California Press, 1968, pp. 394–395.

The Primordialist Approach

The first approach to ethnicity is commonly termed the "primordialist" approach, in that it centers on the assertion that certain primitive (or basic) sociological groupings exist in a society. Such primitive groupings exist a priori, meaning that they are natural units that derive their cohesion from some inherent biological, cultural, or racial traits which then become instruments of social differentiation. The primordial school asserts that human societies are in effect conglomerations of "tribes."[4] The regulating principles that define the distinctions between "tribes" may vary, but what is crucial is that they determine both the boundaries and the meaning of tribal membership in such a way that the "in-group" and "out-group" can always be clearly demarcated. Such a priori existent groupings then constitute the primitive units in society: they define for the individuals within them critical existential distinctions centered on the dichotomy of "us and them"[5] and they perform the crucial task of forming an individual's personal identity through a process of "collective definition."[6] This process, defining the way that "racial groups come to see each other and themselves," is centered on a constant redefinition and reinterpretation of historical events and social experiences vis-à-vis other such groups, and it eventually results in the "aligning and realigning of relations and the development and reformulation of prospective lines of action toward one another."[7] Thus, in the primordialist view, ethnic groups function as insular universes. Their membership is defined by accident of birth, and once constituted, they perpetuate their distinctiveness by a continuing process of socialization that accentuates their perceptions of uniqueness and their sense of separateness from other, similar, social formations.

---

[4]Harold Isaacs, *Idols of the Tribe: Group Identity and Political Change, New* York: Harper Row, 1975, pp. 39–45.

[5]Frederik Barth, "Ethnic Groups and Boundaries," in Frederik Barth (ed.), *Process and Form in Social Life: Selected Essays,* London: Routledge & Kegan Paul, 1981, pp. 198–227.

[6]H. Blumer and T. Duster, "Theories of Race and Social Action," in *Sociological Theories: Race and Colonialism,* Paris: UNESCO, 1980, p. 220.

[7]Ibid., p. 222.

Primordialists and conflict. It is important to recognize that in the primordialist approach, ethnicity is *not* a problematic social category. It is, in fact, almost self-evident, and as a result its theory of conflict is also relatively simple and easy to discern. Although there are as many theories of conflict among the primordialists as there are primordialists themselves, the general logic of conflict generation runs somewhat along the following lines: Ethnic groups are located in pluralist societies that contain several other similar competing social formations. Although relations *within* the ethnic group may be either personal or impersonal in nature, social relations *between* ethnic groups in large societies are invariably impersonal and usually take place through market structures or the political process. These institutions, concerned as they are with the production and distribution of wealth and power, invariably create both winners and losers. To the degree that the winners and losers are congregated disproportionately within some ethnic group, opportunities arise for interaggregational conflict leading to violence. Even if a given ethnic group does not host a disproportionately large number of *objectively* disadvantaged individuals, interaggregational conflict can still occur if, through the process of collective definition, the group internalizes a "myth" of deprivation, thereby channeling internal resentments toward other groups rather than diffusing them within itself. Conflicts as a result of competition over resources certainly could occur even within an ethnic group, but the primordialist assumption—that ethnic groups are characterized by strong forms of organic solidarity flowing from self-evident ties of biology, culture, or race—implies that such competition either would not be significant or would not at any rate result in large-scale violence directed at one's ethnic cohorts. Such significant, large-scale violence would almost by definition be directed primarily at other ethnic groups, justifiably or not, for reasons connected with the larger competitive—tribal—constitution of society.

Primordialists: strengths and weaknesses. The primordialist approach to ethnicity has one important strength, but it suffers from many weaknesses. Its singular strength stems from its focus on factors that easily explain social solidarity. There is little doubt that in many societies, superficial human similarities like pigmentation, hair texture, and other such physical characteristics often serve as elementary justification for simple forms of social solidarity. This solidarity is dependent on a popular belief in a common ancestry based on the notion of "they look like us" and may in fact be reinforced by a common language, common history, and common enemies. Such variables often serve to define a group's identity, but in the primordialist account, they suffice to explain both the nature of group solidarity and how collective action problems are resolved. While primordialist explanations of the former are easier to swallow (especially when group solidarity takes on superficial manifestations and does not involve either high or asymmetrically distributed individual costs), they are less convincing with respect to resolving the collective action problem, except perhaps in the most traditional of societies, or when the "ethnic" groups concerned are extremely small or are in fact simply a form of kinship groups (such as clans).

In all other cases, where a modicum of egoist motivation is combined with the presence of instrumental rationality, the collective action problems inherent in any coordinated group action become more difficult to resolve and cannot be waved away by the simple unproblematic assertion of organic solidarity. This is all the more true because of a glaring empirical problem that contradicts primordialist beliefs, namely, that group identities historically have never been fixed, they are constantly changing, and new identities arise all the time. Moreover, even existing "ethnic" groups contain individuals of varying degrees of common ancestry, they change in composition over time (as in, for example, the creation of the "Anglo-Saxons"), and most important, all ethnic groups have to confront the problem of in-group struggles for power that affect the kind of social solidarity they can amass for purposes of effecting successful collective action. All these factors taken together suggest that the nature of ethnic solidarity is itself highly problematic and cannot be produced as effortlessly on the basis of merely superficial human characteristics, myths of common ancestry, or even a shared history as the primordialist account tends to suggest.

The Epiphenomenalist Approach

In sharp contrast to the primordialist account, which provides an "essentialist" description of the meaning of ethnicity, the second approach, which might be termed the "epiphenomenalist" perspective, denies that "ethnicity" as a *social* phenomenon has any inherent biological basis whatsoever. This approach to ethnicity, evident especially in the Marxist tradition, does not by any means deny the raw existence of physical or social differences ultimately derived from biology and perhaps finally manifested in some specific cultural forms. However, it denies the claim that such biological or cultural formations have an *independent effect, unmediated by class formations or institutional relationships, on politics.*[8] In fact, the epiphenomenalist perspective emphatically asserts that it is the class structures and institutionalized patterns of power in society that are fundamental to explaining political events rather than any biologically or culturally based social formations like "ethnicity." To the degree that "ethnicity" in the primordialist sense plays a role, it functions merely as a "mask" that obscures the identity of some class formations struggling for political or economic power. Ethnicity per se is, therefore, merely an incidental appearance (i.e., "epiphenomenal"): it is not the true, generative, cause of any social phenomenon, even though it often may appear to be.[9]

To the degree that ethnicity appears at all, scholars who accept the epiphenomenalist approach treat it either as a strategy for mobilization on the part of class elites forced to latch on to such means of group identity by pressures of necessity[10] or, especially in Marxist sociology, as a transient form of false consciousness that will be superseded in due time by true class consciousness.[11] In any event, ethnicity in the primordial sense is altogether denied the status of an "efficient cause." It matters primarily as a "label" that identifies different groups placed in relations of cooperation, symbiosis, and conflict based on their location amid the relations of production in a given society.

---

[8]For an excellent survey of Marxist perspectives on race and ethnicity, see John Solomos, "Varieties of Marxist Conceptions of "Race," Class and State: A Critical Analysis," in J. Rex and D. Mason (eds.), *Theories of Race and Ethnic Relations,* Cambridge: Cambridge University Press, 1986, pp. 84–109.

[9]R. Miles, "Marxism Versus the "Sociology of Race Relations?" *Ethnic and Racial Studies,* Vol. 7 (1984), pp. 217–237.

[10]See, for example, J. Rothschild, *Ethnopolitics: A Conceptual Framework,* New York: Columbia University Press, 1981.

[11]See, for example, R. Miles, "Racism, Marxism and British Politics," *Economy and Society,* Vol. 17 (1988), pp. 428–460, and R. Miles, *Racism,* London: Routledge, 1989.

Epiphenomenalists and conflict. The epiphenomenalist approach to "ethnicity" witnessed in Marxist thought was conditioned in part by the fact that Marxism developed within the more or less culturally homogeneous capitalist societies of Western Europe, where class relations rather than ethnic formations become a natural focus for theory. However, when Marxist ideas spread to more ethnically heterogeneous societies beyond Europe, the issue of ethnicity as a factor in social action had to be addressed anew. It was only then that theorists provided the definitive reading that integrated ethnicity, as understood by the primordialists, within the larger Marxist theme of generalized class struggle. Such integration in effect denied that ethnicity could ever be an independent element disturbing the normal, conflictual dynamics in capitalist society, but it did point to three critical features as part of its theory of conflict that any model seeking to assess the prospects for ethnic violence must confront. The Marxist theory of social conflict is too comprehensive and too well-known to merit being summarized here. However, three insights with respect to ethnicity are worth reiterating.

First, any scrutiny of ethnicity with respect to political mobilization would do well to examine the prevailing means and relations of production existing in any society. Such an examination would identify differential, and perhaps exploitative, patterns of distribution of wealth and power and thus suggest potential "class" groupings that might manifest themselves under certain conditions through "ethnic" terms.

Second, the role of the state in "reproducing" ethnicity is crucial.[12] This implies that the state apparatus may simply preserve what appears to be certain "ethnically" structured patterns of exploitation. Such patterns may be obvious and may even be defined "ethnically" (as in the case of apartheid in South Africa), but they are more accurately part of a larger effort at maintaining the economic power of a certain class rather than merely "ideological" conflicts between certain biologically grouped social formations. Under certain conditions, the state may create "ethnicity" as a vehicle of political mobilization. The state may even embark on such efforts in order to assert

[12]See the discussion in Michael Omi and Howard Winant, *Racial Formation in the United States,* New York: Routledge & Kegan Paul, 1986.

its own autonomy against certain dominant classes or with an eye to bolstering its prospects for survival against incipiently rising challengers.

Third, "ethnic" violence is invariably (or, at least, often enough) a product of class antagonisms or of class-state antagonism. This implies that ethnic violence is often more than it appears to be. Very rarely is it—journalistic predilections to the contrary—an accidental or irrational outcome caused either by passions getting out of hand, or the "madness of crowds," or differences in outlooks rooted in religion, *weltanschauung*, or other cultural differences. While such ingredients may constitute the proximate cause of violence in any given situation, the roots of the violence lie in fissures deep beneath the surface—fissures that more often than not are strongly connected with serious and consequential contentions about the distribution of wealth and resources.

Epiphenomenalists: strengths and weaknesses. The "epiphenomenal" approach to ethnicity has many strengths but one important weakness. Its principal strength lies in the fact that it draws attention to politics as a struggle for wealth and profit. Consequently, it provides a fairly coherent account as to why certain empirical groupings can coalesce politically and how they can act collectively with respect to the ongoing competition for resources. Instead of making an a priori claim of biological or cultural affinity to explain such solidarity, the epiphenomenalist perspective accounts for the solidarity by individual self-interest combined with differential access to the means of production. The epiphenomenalist view thus paves the way for viewing "ethnicity" not as a permanent characteristic of individuals, but as an incidental coloration that may or may not acquire salience depending on the circumstances confronting the process of mobilization. If "ethnicity" becomes salient, however, it can be understood as part of a larger structural competition that engages both interclass and class-state relations. By focusing on these critical arenas of social action, the epiphenomenal view reminds the analyst about the constant struggle for resources in any society and, accordingly, provides a means of contextualizing "ethnic" struggles within the larger realm of social competition.

The epiphenomenal perspective represents a useful corrective to the "essentialist" approach favored by the primordialists, but it has one important weakness, namely its reliance on a single explanatory variable, such as class in the Marxist approach. This focus on a single variable precludes an analysis of ethnicity as a phenomenon in its own right. While the importance of ethnicity as an independent causal factor may in fact be small (and Marxism has done more than perhaps any other system of analysis to establish this conclusion), the extent of its contribution and the nature of its appearance in any given case can only be discerned empirically. As such, it still merits independent examination, if for no other reason than the multitude of sins attributed to it. Marxism, however, has few tools to conduct such an examination, since it simply subsumes "ethnicity" under a wider set of social relations or merely treats it as a superstructural phenomenon hiding the "true" base.[13]

The Ascriptive Approach

The third approach to ethnicity overcomes the limitations of both the primordial and the Marxist perspectives while retaining the best elements of both traditions. This approach, which can be dubbed "ascriptive" and derives from the work of Max Weber and scholars who have followed him, is distinguished by a view of ethnicity that is best described as *real, but constructed.* Weber's discontent with the "multiple social origins and theoretical ambiguities"[14] of ethnicity as a concept has been alluded to earlier, but despite his arguments about the "disutility of the notion of the 'ethnic group,'"[15] he defined the latter carefully enough to make productive analysis possible. Ethnic groups, according to Weber, are

> those human groups that entertain a subjective belief in their common descent because of similarities of physical type or of customs or both, or because of memories of colonization and migration. This belief must be important for the propagation of group formation; conversely, it does not matter whether or not an objective blood relationship exists.[16]

---

[13]Solomos, op. cit.

[14]Weber, *Economy and Society*, p. 387.

[15]Ibid., p. 393.

[16]Ibid., p. 389.

The key distinguishing mark of ethnicity in this reading is the notion of "subjective belief," that is, the animating conviction held by members of a group that they do enjoy a common ancestry and hence are bound together by some ineffable tie that in truth may be wholly fictitious. Thanks to this belief, "ethnic membership differs from the kinship group precisely by being a *presumed identity*...."[17] This insistence on presumed identity as the structuring principle of ethnic unity does *not* imply, however, any particular consequences for social and political action. In fact, Weber insistently argues that "ethnic membership does *not* constitute a group; it only facilitates group formation of any kind, particularly in the political sphere."[18]

Weber's general approach thus consists of the affirmation that ethnic groupings can exist as a result of certain mythical intersubjective beliefs held by a collectivity, but their mere existence does not have any *necessary* consequences for social action. To the degree that the latter phenomenon needs to be explained, the explanations must be found elsewhere. Through such a "constructivist" approach Weber manages to solve the vexing problem afflicting both the primordialist and epiphenomenalist traditions in that he suggests how "ethnicity" can be treated as a causative variable without allowing it to dominate the explanatory space. As described earlier, the primordialist asks for too much, while the epiphenomenalist gives away too little. The former treats ethnicity as a self-evident fact that automatically explains all manner of collective action; in contrast, the latter treats ethnicity as merely an incidental appearance that can be readily and completely discarded in favor of more consequential, though hidden, social forces.

Weber carves an artful middle ground. He allows for the possibility that ethnicity can be created ("ascribed"), even if only through the collective imagination of apparently similar individuals. In so doing, he could be said to accept an insight that has roots in the primordialist tradition. But he does not make the fact of ethnic groups arising determinative for any social acts. Thus he allows for the possibility that precisely those kinds of forces identified by the epiphenomenalists might be among the real drivers beneath what are otherwise

[17]Ibid. Emphasis added.

[18]Ibid.

taken to be "ethnic" phenomena. In fact, he broadens the epiphenomenalist insight still further. Instead of restricting himself merely to the class dynamics seen to operate in capitalist societies (which Marxists would assert represent the real movers beneath "ethnic" action), Weber would suggest that the compulsions of politics—understood as the struggle for power writ large—explain the origins and persistence of groups and cause them to discover a variety of solidarity-producing myths like ethnicity. Thus, he notes that "it is primarily the political community, no matter how artificially organized, that inspires the belief in common ethnicity. This belief tends to persist even after the disintegration of the political community, unless drastic differences in the custom, physical type, or, above all, language exist among its members."[19]

Ascriptivists and conflict. The above passage makes clear the ascriptive approach to ethnicity: Politics creates ethnicity in that it forces individuals to discover common resources in their struggles for survival.[20] The fundamental role of politics implies that ethnicity as a phenomenon becomes real only because of the subjective constructions of individuals under certain circumstances and not because it exists a priori as some intrinsically permanent solidarity binding a set of individuals across time and space. Such a perspective, then, provokes a set of questions that demand further investigation by any model seeking to anticipate ethnic strife. First, what factors precipitate the generation of these intersubjective beliefs relating to ethnicity? Second, how do these beliefs, once generated, come to precipitate group mobilization and possibly collective action? And third, how do state actions—which, as the Marxists correctly point out, are critical to reproducing ethnicity—contribute to group definition, mobilization, and possibly violent social action? Weber's sociology and the scholars working in his tradition provide pointers that direct the search for answers to these questions. Three key insights stand out in this regard.

---

[19]Ibid.

[20]In some sense, the discovery of such associations is a "natural" process because "if rationally regulated action is not widespread, almost any association, even the most rational one, creates an overarching communal consciousness; this takes the form of a brotherhood on the basis of the belief in common ethnicity." Weber, *Economy and Society*, p. 389.

First, Weber draws attention to power and domination as the central, fundamental features of politics, the latter understood as that activity relating to the production of order in social life. Domination, in fact, "constitutes a special case of power"[21] and in a general sense describes all the mechanisms concerned with "imposing one's own will upon the behavior of other persons."[22] When viewed in such terms, domination becomes "one of the most important elements of social action," and although "not every form of social action reveals a structure of dominancy," it plays a considerable role in all varieties of social action, including the economic, "even where it is not obvious at first sight."[23] The key insight residing here, accordingly, is the claim that politics is central to the regulation of social life. Politics subsumes economics, and to that extent, the quest for domination that drives all political life appears in the economic realm as well: "economic power, is a frequent, often purposefully willed, consequence of domination as well as one of its most important instruments."[24] Because domination is so central to political, economic, and even social structures, any theoretical model that seeks to understand the generation of ethnicity *must* focus on how individuals attempt to structure patterns of domination in political communities, and such structuring of domination must be investigated both with respect to the in-group and the political community at large.[25]

Second, since the struggle for domination lies at the heart of all community life, it brings in its trail efforts at monopolizing power. These attempts at monopolizing power occur both within groups and in society at large in an interactive and often mutually reinforcing fashion. Weber described these dynamics by the phrase "monopolistic closure,"[26] which refers to all efforts made at preventing "others" from sharing in the political, economic, and social bounties enjoyed by a few. These efforts can occur in different ways,

---

[21]Weber, *Economy and Society*, Vol. 2, p. 941.

[22]Ibid., p. 942.

[23]Ibid., p. 941.

[24]Ibid., p. 942.

[25]For a pioneering theoretical analysis of how such patterns of domination are manifested at multiple levels, see Frank Parkin, *Marxism and Class Theory: A Bourgeois Critique*, New York: Columbia University Press, 1979.

[26]Weber, *Economy and Society*, p. 388.

depending on historical and social circumstances. They may begin as small confederate efforts mounted by a few individuals to capture power, wealth, or social status. Such efforts would be designed to keep "others" out merely to maximize the distributed share of acquired gains. If these strategies are successful and in fact come to be institutionalized in ethnic terms throughout the polity, they would represent forms of "outside pressures" which in turn could impel disadvantaged individuals to search for other ideational devices to generate responding forms of resistance. The way these patterns of closure *originate* is less interesting than the fact that they do exist pervasively in all societies: dominant groups use them to keep others out; successful but still relatively disadvantaged groups use them to prevent a dilution of their gains; and utterly disadvantaged individuals tend to use them to recover a modicum of solidarity, which makes resistance and the pursuit of revanchist strategies possible.[27]

Third, the criteria for justifying individual or group efforts at monopolizing power do not have to be objectively defensible. What is important to recognize when exclusion is attempted by any groups in ethnic terms is that "*any* cultural trait, no matter how superficial, can serve as a starting point for the familiar tendency to monopolistic closure."[28] Often, "it does not matter which characteristic is chosen in the individual case: whatever suggests itself most easily is seized upon." Consequently, theoretical models seeking to understand the generation of ethnicity must go beyond proximate ideational labels to scrutinize those underlying structures of domination and deprivation in the political, economic, and social realms that make recourse to such labels relevant.

Ascriptivists: strengths and weaknesses. The ascriptive approach is attractive because of its multiple strengths. Its primary strength is that it is an open-ended approach: it provides a means of viewing ethnicity that allows for the integration of "primordialist" and "epiphenomenalist" insights but does not force the analysis into any single predetermined hypothesis. It identifies core issues that must be engaged—like the instrumental nature of ethnic phenomena, the

---

[27]This notion of "dual closure" is examined in some detail in Parkin, op. cit., pp. 89–116.

[28]Weber, op. cit., p. 388.

pervasiveness of domination, and the ubiquity of overt and covert forms of social closure—but it leaves the analyst free to incorporate these factors into any causal hypothesis of his own choosing. Thus, it opens the door for the incorporation of insights deriving from resource competition, rational choice, and symbolic interactionist approaches to ethnicity.[29] Further, it assumes the premise of methodological individualism. It makes rational individuals the theoretical primates for purposes of social explanation, even as it can accommodate macroscopic entities like "ethnic groups" for analytical purposes. Being centered on individuals with specifically attributed preferences and capabilities, it avoids the problems of reification that arise from the use of ungenerated macroscopic wholes. Because of its flexibility, the approach lacks the easily identifiable flaws of the other two approaches.

RATIONALE FOR USING THE ASCRIPTIVE APPROACH

For all the reasons examined above, the ascriptive approach to ethnicity is the most defensible approach to developing a model for anticipating ethnic violence. This approach may in fact be vehemently repudiated by ethnic activists, since such individuals often have a deep stake in primordialist conceptions of ethnicity. Similarly, those with a stake in doctrinaire ideological explanations of social relations may also deny the validity of an ascriptive approach. But most social theorists today would admit that an ascriptive approach incorporating both Marxist and Weberian insights is the most fruitful avenue to understanding the larger problem of exclusion and domination in society.[30]

In light of the above discussion of various competing approaches, ethnicity may be defined as the idea of shared group affinity and belonging based on the myth of common ancestry and a notion of distinctiveness. The group in question must be larger than a kinship group, but the sense of belonging—based on myth—stems from cre-

---

[29]Several of these approaches with respect to ethnicity are detailed in Rex and Mason, op. cit.

[30]An excellent example of this claim may be found in V. Burris, "The Neo-Marxist Synthesis of Marx and Weber on Class," in N. Wiley (ed.), *The Marx-Weber Debate*, Newbury Park: Sage, 1987, pp. 67–90.

ated bonds that have close similarities to kinship. The basis for these created bonds may stem from any number of distinguishing characteristics, such as race, language, religion, or regional differentiation. These are, at any rate, incidental and case-specific, but when created they often result in deep, almost fanatical, personal attachments. So it is probably not a coincidence that when ethnic conflict results in societies in which kinship and ethnicity play a dominant and pervasive role in social relations, it often takes on an extremely cruel edge.[31]

---

[31]This usage of the term "ethnicity "is based on Donald L. Horowitz, *Ethnic Groups in Conflict,* Los Angeles: University of California Press, 1985, who derives his conception from the larger ascriptive tradition associated with Weber.

Toward a Model for Anticipating Ethnic Violence

OUTLINE OF THE MODEL

The conceptual model for anticipating ethnic violence described in this section focuses on how the grievances stemming from existing patterns of domination and deprivation in any society could be translated into imperatives for group mobilization, which in turn interact with various state actions to produce a variety of political outcomes ranging from political reconciliation to state breakdown. This approach attempts to understand the dynamics of group definition, ethnic mobilization, strategic bargaining, and political action as part of a single continuous process.

Taking its cues from the ascriptive tradition, the model approaches ethnicity primarily as a "marker," that is, as a real but constructed instrument for defining group identity as a prelude to collective mobilization and social action. Thus, the approach seeks to accommodate insights from both the primordial and epiphenomenal schools: It accepts that ethnicity can be used to identify certain social formations, and that ethnicity in this sense can derive from *any* perceived commonalties such as race, language, religion, geographic origins, or culture, in addition to more direct affinities derived from kinship. However, it presumes that such ethnic markers arise principally against a backdrop of ongoing social struggles, which may have conspicuous economic components but are not necessarily restricted to them.

The resulting model, graphically illustrated in Figure A.1, focuses on the dynamics of mobilization for the purposes of highlighting the three basic issues critical to the outbreak of ethnically based violence. First, what is the structural potential for strife? Second, what are the requirements for potential strife to be transformed into likely strife? Third, how does likely strife degenerate into actual strife? In attempting to address these three issues, the model identifies three bilateral interactions. Each successive interaction builds on the foregoing one in an effort to typify the generative process describing the dynamics of ethnic violence.

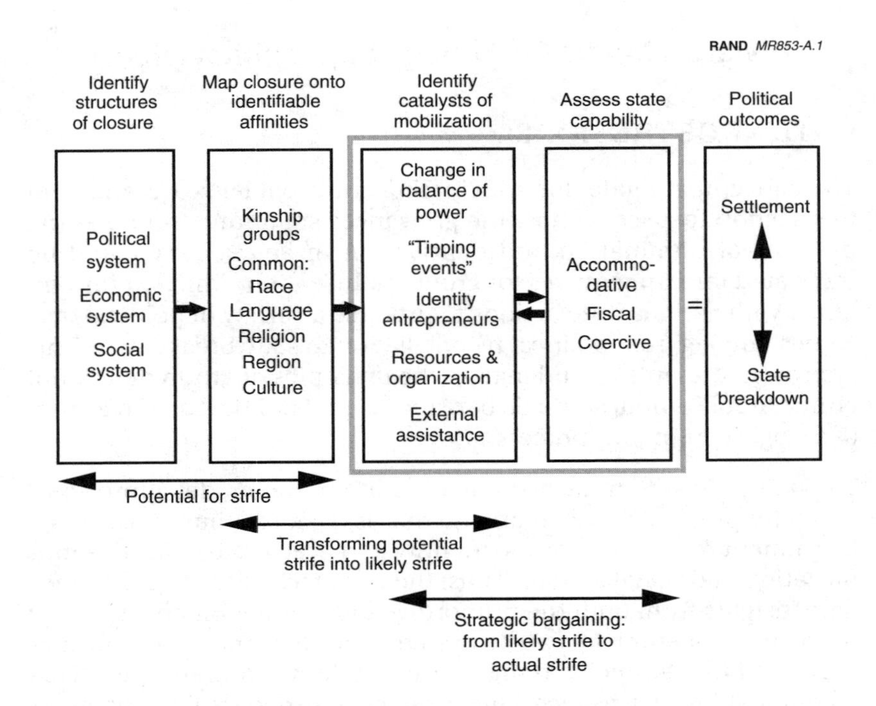

Figure A.1—Anticipating Ethnic Conflict

STAGE I

Investigating the Potential for Strife

Closure. The first issue the model seeks to address is the structural potential for strife. Consistent with the ascriptive tradition, it seeks to determine this potential for strife by investigating a given society's patterns of closure. The Weberian concept of closure, which is central here, refers to the "process of subordination whereby one group monopolizes advantages by closing off opportunities to another group."[32] Closure theorists distinguish between two main and reciprocal modes of closure: exclusionary and usurpationary.

---

[32]Raymond Murphy, *Social Closure: The Theory of Monopolization and Exclusion*, Oxford: Clarendon Press, 1988, p. 8.

Exclusionary closure involves the exercise of power in a downward direction, when one group attempts to secure its advantages by closing off the opportunities available to another group by treating it as inferior or ineligible. Usurpationary closure involves the exercise of power in an upward direction, as for example when subordinate groups attempt to erode the advantages of higher groups.[33] Both modes represent means for mobilizing power to enhance or defend a group's share of rewards or resources. Because the struggle for power is constant in any society, the justification for exclusion as embodied in various forms of closure is always open to challenge, and the public arena constantly witnesses efforts to make the boundaries between dominator and dominated either obscure or transparent, legitimate or illegitimate.[34] And since the state ultimately rationalizes the legal terms of closure and domination, it becomes the central arena where the processes of exclusion and usurpation unfold.

The three realms of closure. The three arenas of critical importance for the purposes of examining closure are the political, the economic, and the social. The political arena relates to all matters of governance, administrative control, and command over the means of coercion. The economic arena relates to all matters connected with the production of wealth and the distribution of resources. The social arena relates to all matters connected with the effective claims on social esteem, including the distribution of status and social privileges.

Each of these arenas demarcates a particular dimension of the public order and each is related in multiple ways to the others, but constrictions in the political realm are perhaps the most important form of closure for purposes of establishing the potential for strife. The political realm has such primacy because the issue of who rules, and how, directly affects all kinds of outcomes within the polity.[35]

---

[33]Ibid., pp. 8–10. The concepts of exclusionary and usurpationary closure were originally developed by Parkin, op. cit.

[34]Murphy, op. cit., p. 48.

[35]See the discussion in James Buchanan and Gordon Tullock, *The Calculus of Consent,* Ann Arbor: University of Michigan Press, 1962.

To begin with, political authority literally holds the power of life and death over its citizenry as a result of its monopolistic claim on the means of coercion and the legitimacy normally accorded to its ability to employ force. This power is usually exercised through myriad tools of domestic law enforcement, direct political action against individuals and groups, and through organized state efforts at staving off political disorder. Consequently, the nature of political authority and state structure affects the primary interest of individuals—survival—in a very direct, and often unmediated, way. The political realm also has primacy because it embodies the "rules of the game." It represents the differential and regulated access to power afforded to different groups as well as control over the ability to amend these rules of access.

Finally, the political realm enjoys primacy because it can control—through force if necessary—both rules and outcomes in the economic and social realms. To be sure, economic power often provides the buttress for political power, but it is usually indirect and not highly visible in its effects. At any rate, holders of economic power cannot survive direct competition with political authority, except by recourse to political means. For this reason, economic power holders generally seek to operate in arenas relatively autonomous from state action or attempt to ally with holders of political power for survival and domination.

The social realm is probably the least salient of the three arenas, except perhaps in traditional societies. Because status monopolies usually derive from vocational origins, hereditary charisma, or hierocratic claims, the social realm in nontraditional societies usually acquires importance only when the status groups within it are linked to larger loci of economic or political power. Indeed, the derivative nature of the social realm is often evident from the fact that politically or economically advantaged groups tend to have a high social status.

Despite the centrality of the political realm, assessing the potential for strife requires identifying patterns of asymmetrical relative power and domination in all three realms. This is done not only to develop a particular profile of a given country or region, but also to identify in advance which sets of individuals might coalesce, form alliances of convenience, or become pointed antagonists as the process of ethnic mobilization evolves over time. Which of these behaviors will actually occur cannot be predicted a priori, in the absence of additional information about the preferences and capabilities of each of these groups, but the very fact of identifying the relevant actors and their location vis-à-vis each other already provides some means of anticipating how different group interactions may evolve over time.

Identifying Closure

Keeping in mind that the principal objective of the first stage of the model is to identify the prevailing structures of closure in the political, economic, and social realms, there are two important variables in each of these arenas: (1) the existing patterns of distribution with respect to power, wealth, and status respectively, and (2) the relative ease with which individuals can secure access to power, wealth, and status through peaceful means. Each of these variables is important in different ways. The first variable depicts a static picture of existing patterns of dominance and deprivation, whereas the second speaks to a more dynamic issue, namely the possibilities for peaceful change.

The political realm. At the level of the political system, scrutinizing the existing distribution of power requires assessing the composition of the principal political authorities in the country with respect to their subnational categories like race, language, religion, region, or culture. Such an assessment requires sensitivity to the nature of the political regime and to the question of unitary (one-branch) or divided (multibranch) government. If the government is unitary, attention should be focused primarily on the executive and bureaucratic arms of the state. This requires scrutinizing the composition of the executive decisionmaking elite (whether civilian or military) as well as the upper echelons of the bureaucracy. The former consists mainly of ministerial-equivalent positions and above, whereas the latter relates to director-level positions and above in the civilian bureaucracy and to colonel-equivalents and their superiors in the military and internal security-police bureaucracies.

To the degree that state structure is characterized by divided rather than unitary government, the width of relevant focus groups would have to be expanded. The composition of legislative and judicial bodies might also have to be scrutinized in the context of understanding both the nature of, and the constraints imposed on, the exercise of power in such divided governments. A special circumstance arises in federal states. Because of the devolution of central power implied by a federal setup, in such cases an examination of the type suggested above is warranted both at the state and the regional (provincial) levels.

Assembling raw compositional data on how the institutions singled out above are manned in any form of government provides a valuable sociological profile of a state (or province). But such information by itself does not confirm the extent of political closure within the polity. To derive such an assessment, it is important to relate the compositional data about the leadership population to its relative size within the population as a whole. In other words, the actual proportion of political elites measured by subnational categories like race, language, religion, region, or culture should be compared with the size of such demographic categories within the population as a whole. Such a comparison of actual representation vis-à-vis some notionally appropriate number derived from proportional representation may provide some clues about the level of political closure.

An understanding of the *possible* extent of political closure needs to be complemented by an assessment of whether the state in question pursues a formal agenda of closure aimed at restricting the participation of some groups in political life. This is important because institutional designs and structures have a fundamental bearing on whether patterns of closure derived from numerical comparisons are in fact significant, spurious, or merely accidental. Accordingly, there is a need for additional information about the second variable identified earlier, namely, the relative ease with which individuals can secure access to power through peaceful means. This implies examining whether there are formal or informal restrictions on political participation; whether there is universal access to a system for peacefully redressing grievances; whether ruling institutions and groups subject themselves to periodic, peaceful, tests of legitimacy; and whether there is a viable civil society. Information about such dynamic elements of access to power is crucial if one is to judge the nature and extent of political closure. Often such information may not be quantifiable, although several attempts at quantifying the degree of responsiveness within a political system already exist.[36] Nonetheless, such information is necessary and must be related to other numeric data on representation if a better and clearer understanding of the patterns of political closure within a given society is to be derived. The patterns derived from the first examination might serve as a tip-off for an examination of the formal rules of closure and exclusion that may exist in the society.

The economic realm. A similar scrutiny is necessary in the economic realm. Here too, the focus rests on identifying first the general patterns of the way wealth is distributed as well as the relative institutional freedom of access to resources existing within the polity. The overall pattern of distributed wealth and income provides an important clue with respect to the issue of economic closure.[37] The objective again is first to assemble data that identify how income and property are distributed at the elite and general population levels, with the data categorized by reference to certain substate categories like race, language, religion, region, or culture within a given country. The data then must be related proportionally to the relevant demographic categories in the population as a whole (just as in the political data, misrepresentation of demographic categories is likely in many societies). The rationale for advocating analysis at the economic realm at both the elite and the general population levels is to cross-check for the accuracy of the patterns.

The information then must be complemented by perhaps more important qualitative information about institutional structures and about individuals' relative access to economic resources. For example, are there any formal or informal restrictions on investment, trade, business, and employment directed at particular groups categorized by the substate categories described earlier? Such restrictions, coupled with quantitative data on the distribution of wealth and income, would provide powerful evidence of serious economic closure with consequent implications for the potential for strife.

---

[36]The annual surveys produced by Freedom House, Amnesty International, etc. are examples of such efforts.

[37]See the discussion in Manus I. Mildarsky, "Rulers and Ruled: Patterned Inequality and the Onset of Mass Political Violence," *American Political Science Review*, Vol. 82 (1988), pp. 491–509.

If the state's economy is not predominantly market oriented but has command features in varying degrees, the second issue of relative freedom of access to resources intersects more clearly with political mechanisms of closure and becomes all the more important. A command economy concentrates wealth in the hands of state managers who can embark on exclusionary distribution schemes in a much more explicit and organized fashion than market mechanisms can. If the principles of exclusion in such arrangements are defined either explicitly or implicitly by certain substate categories like race, language, religion, region, or culture, the problems of economic closure may be much more intractable, with more serious implications for potential strife.

The social realm. The analysis carried out with respect to the political and economic realms must be extended to the social realm as well, but by necessity, the terms of reference vary in this arena. The key issue to be examined with respect to the social realm is the extent of the effective claims made on social esteem and the forms in which these claims translate into differentially distributed but tangible economic and political benefits. Specifically, the examination must focus on whether the given country has status groups based on vocation (i.e., differential standing based on occupation), hereditary charisma (i.e., differential standing based on successful claims of higher-ranking descent), or some version of hierocratic or historical claims (i.e., differential standing based either on religious vocation or specific universally recognized historical actions or through secular claims associated with national embodiment groups). In the last category, a common example is the status differential accorded to some groups on the basis of a claim to the national idea, contrasted with groups that may be seen as foreign and having arrived through immigration. Irrespective of their origins, the size of the status groups needs to be established and the nature and extent of their social claims assessed. The task provides an understanding of the social profile of the state, including a preliminary judgment about the relative power of various dominant and pariah groups within the country.

Just as in political and economic realms, a static measure of the size and capabilities of the status group is insufficient for purposes of discerning the extent and robustness of social closure. To gauge such dimensions qualitatively, other questions have to be addressed: How rigid are the extant forms of status stratification? How controversial are the existing norms of stratification? What kinds of social mobility are possible, and what is the extent of such mobility? Are the tangible benefits accruing to members claiming different kinds of social status merely symbolic, or are they substantive and disproportionate relative to the tangible social contributions perceived to be made by the status groups in question? Focusing on such questions would provide a better sense of how status groups in the social realm intersect with the political and economic structures of power, thereby laying the basis for a clearer idea of the potential for strife.

Summarizing the notion of closure. The overall purpose of the scrutiny of the political, economic, and social system is designed to do three things: (1) to provide a general profile of which sets of individuals either benefit most or are deprived most by the prevailing social structures when classified by certain substatal categories like race, language, religion, region, or culture; (2) to identify the level of disproportion in the dominance or deprivation of the given group relative to its size or standing in the population as a whole; and (3) to assess the opportunities for peaceful transformation in the system as a whole by means of a systematic scrutiny of the existing institutional structures, the ruling norms of behavior, and the general expectations about appropriate political actions. Taken together, such an examination, conducted skillfully, might suggest whether significant forms of closure exist in any given country.

If significant forms of closure are discovered, it still would be premature to claim that "ethnic" strife is probable. For such a claim to be sustained, the burdens of closure must be shown to fall disproportionately on individuals with certain potential affinities. That is, individuals who share possible solidarity deriving from race, language, religion, regional origin, or culture must either be objectively disadvantaged as a result of such closure—whether they know it or not—or they must be capable of being "conscientized" on the basis of some such affinity in the presence of specific perceptions of deprivation. In such circumstances, it does not matter if the basis for affinity is entirely spurious, for so long as the fact of deprivation (or the appearance thereof) can be shown to fall on individuals potentially linked by "some externally identifiable characteristic,"[38] the potential for usurpation and strife by disadvantaged individuals can be said to exist. Therefore, the first stage of the model illustrated above is completed by a systematic effort at mapping out previously identified patterns of closure onto potential affinities centered either on kinship groups or other forms of presumed identity based on race, language, religion, geographic origin, or culture.

STAGE II

Understanding the Transformation from Potential to Likely Strife

Potential versus likely strife. Establishing the potential for strife is not the same as establishing the likelihood of strife. If objective patterns of closure exist within a given state and if they burden certain sets of individuals with identifiable affinities, the potential for strife certainly exists. Transforming that potential into likely strife, however, requires certain catalytic elements. The necessity of a catalyst is particularly salient because large-scale social violence, especially that involving coordinated actions by numerous individuals, rarely (if ever) occurs as a result of spontaneous social combustion. The claim that violent action often derives from the perceived "feeling that prevailing conditions limit or hinder"[39] the political prospects of individuals is often rooted in the classical imagery of Jacobin revolutions, which depicted social uprisings as deriving from simultaneous, unconnected, and spontaneous actions by large numbers of discontented individuals. Such a vision received its most sophisticated treatment in the early work of revolution theorists like James Davies and Ted Robert Gurr, who argued that the prospects for large-scale violence are linked primarily to the conditions of unbearable immiserization. As Gurr succinctly described the thesis, "the more widespread and intense deprivation is among members of the population, the greater is the magnitude of strife in one or another

[38]Weber, op. cit., p. 342.

[39]Crane Brinton, *The Anatomy of Revolution,* New York: Harper and Row, 1965, p. 33.

form."[40] However, neither Gurr nor Davies argues in favor of a simple relationship between deprivation and strife. Both analysts employ intervening variables that center mostly on the capacity of the system to satisfy individual or group expectations. For example, Davies argues that although immiserization sets the stage for revolutionary events, they are most likely to occur "when a prolonged period of objective economic and social development is followed by a short period of sharp reversal."[41] In Davies's logic, such a pattern arises because individual expectations do not decrease in proportion to the state's decrease in institutional capacity; large-scale social violence is a result of rising expectations amidst declining satisfactions. Despite such sophisticated hypothesizing, the core argument still remains fairly simple: relative deprivation, though mediated, constitutes the principal cause of likely strife.

The main problem with such an argument is that it need not be true. To begin with, the deprivation experienced by a given population may not lead to strife or even to opposition if the bonds of solidarity within the affected groups are merely latent or fractured. The latter possibility is particularly relevant because modern societies invariably place individuals in multiple roles. Individuals may acquire multiple identities conditioned both by the various activities they engage in and the different levels and kinds of meaning bequeathed by their membership in diverse social formations. There may also be cross-cutting cleavages in society that keep groups from coalescing along certain specific lines despite the existence of otherwise widespread deprivation. The existence of multiple identities and cross-cutting cleavages can, therefore, conspire to prevent relative deprivation from resulting in an increased propensity for strife.

Nevertheless, it is important to recognize that deprivational approaches highlight an important kernel of truth: the existence of deprivation is, as Gurr puts it, "the basic condition for civil strife of any kind."[42] Consequently, the deprivational approaches are not false,

---

[40]Ted Robert Gurr, "A Causal Model of Civil Strife: A Comparative Analysis Using New Indices," *American Political Science Review*, Vol. 62 (1968), p. 1105.

[41]James Davies, "Toward a Theory of Revolution," *American Sociological Review*, Vol. 6 (1962), p. 5.

[42]Gurr, op. cit., p. 1105.

simply incomplete.[43] They tell only a part of the story. Their core concerns about inequality, disinheritance, and alienation need to be integrated with other elements that can transform these dispositions into "joint action in pursuit of common ends."[44] This implies connecting the "diffuse strains and discontents within the population" with a "central political process" so that ethnic-based collective action can be seen for what it actually is: a species of political action in which "specific claims and counter-claims [are] made on the existing [regime] by various mobilized groups" in order to secure "established places within the [extant] structure of power."[45] Or, to put it in terms favored by closure theorists, political guidance and organization are needed to transform diffuse dissatisfaction into effective usurpationary action.

The ethnic ingredient by itself never obliterates the basic fact that all such collective actions simply amount to forms of political mobilization designed to capture power or increase the extent of power already possessed. Consequently, any violence that may accompany mobilization is always political violence, which in turn is "essentially a by-product of [the] omnipresent process of political conflict among mobilized—that is, organized and resource controlling—groups and governments."[46] This argument highlights the complementary dimensions—organized mobilization and reactive state action—necessary to complete the deprivationist narrative and to transform it into a coherent theory about ethnic violence because, as Aya remarked, "for all the violent passion and passionate violence they entail, revolutions, rebellion, and lesser forms of coercive civilian conflict are

[43]Gurr's early version of relative deprivation theory was tested and rejected, primarily on this basis. Stephen G. Brush, "Dynamics of Theory Change in the Social Sciences; Relative Deprivation and Collective Violence," *Journal of Conflict Resolution,* Vol. 40, No. 4 (1996), pp. 523–545.

[44]Charles Tilly, *From Mobilization to Revolution,* Reading: Addison-Wesley, 1978, p. 84.

[45]Charles Tilly, "Does Modernization Breed Revolution?" *Comparative Politics,* Vol. 5, No. 3 (1973), p. 436.

[46]Theda Skocpol, "France, Russia, China: A Structural Analysis of Social Revolutions," *Comparative Studies in Society and History,* Vol. 18, No. 2 (1976), p. 165.

best understood as (to adopt Clausewitz's venerable definition of war) 'a mere continuation of politics by other means.'"[47]

Mobilization for Political Action

Understanding how individuals who are potentially motivated as a result of deprivation become *mobilized* in the form of "ethnic" groups constitutes the core of Stage II of the model illustrated earlier. Five factors are critical to this process.

Incipient changes in the balance of power. The first factor consists simply of any significant—incipient—changes in the prevailing patterns of closure or the existing balance of power within a state and sometimes outside it. Since all polities are constantly in flux, thanks to the myriad changes taking place in the political, economic, and social dimensions of public life, social change is clearly as inevitable as it often is mundane. These changes, usually arising out of the normal processes of politics and economics, tend to occur constantly but in incremental form. As such, they rarely incur concentrated attention. Every so often, however, a set of dramatic social changes appear poised to materialize: these changes almost take the form of "step functions" as opposed to the merely accretional modifications constantly witnessed in public life. Changes of this kind can be deliberate, as for example when certain political or constitutional alterations threaten to transform the prevailing patterns of power and privilege; or they can be merely a consequence of an evolutionary process, as for example when certain economic groups finally begin to realize supernormal profits from previously marginally successful ventures; or they can be simply accidental, as for example when the discovery of new resources suddenly increases the wealth of formerly peripheral property owners, or where defeat in an interstate war changes the power relations existing within a given country.

No matter how such changes occur, the critical issue from the point of view of anticipating mobilization is that such changes must be, first, significant in absolute terms and, more importantly, capable of causing significant alterations in the prevailing internal balances of

---

[47]Roderick Aya, "Theories of Revolution Reconsidered: Contrasting Models of Collective Violence," *Theory and Society*, Vol. 8, No. 1 (1979), p. 68.

power. In other words, the changes worthy of attention are not the mundane changes that constantly occur in social life but the ones that threaten to *immediately* alter the extant patterns of closure in a given society. The prospect of immediate change is critical from the point of view of mobilization, because social changes that threaten to alter the prevailing patterns of power over the long run—no matter how significant they are and how clearly they are foreseen by the perspicacious—usually do not result in collective action, for two main reasons. First, individuals tend to discount the future and as such are less motivated to respond to contingencies that do not threaten their immediate interests. Second, the very length of time required to make long-run changes effective usually implies that many other alternative outcomes could obtain and hence serve to retard pressures for social mobilization and collective action.

The prospect of significant and immediate changes in the prevailing patterns of social closure, however, is the perfect precipitant of collective action, and it can work in one of two ways. To begin with, it can catalyze expectations of quick success and thereby motivate individuals who are dissatisfied with the prevailing balances of power to increase their individual efforts toward group mobilization based on potential solidarities like race, language, regional origin, or culture. The prospect of incipient change in existing forms of social closure can also work in the opposite direction, in that it can result in collective action by individuals threatened with imminent loss of power or privilege. While there is no reason—in terms of the principles of standard utility theory—why individuals threatened by loss should behave any differently from individuals in pursuit of gains, there is some experimental evidence to suggest that individuals faced with the prospect of significant, immediate losses tend to be more risk acceptant and, by implication, might be willing to bear greater burdens—if necessary, in the form of enhanced contributions to collective action—in the hope of avoiding such losses. This evidence, captured in conceptual terms by "prospect theory,"[48] would suggest that fear among the privileged of immediate loss *might* result in more effective collective action—perhaps expressed in ethnic id-

---

[48]The classic formulation can be found in Daniel Kahneman and Amos Tvesky, "Prospect Theory: An Analysis of Decision Under Risk," *Econometrica,* Vol. 47, No. 2 (March 1979), pp. 263–291.

ioms—if such an outcome promises to avert the anticipated losses. The direction in which the pressures toward mobilization run is less important than the factors that cause the pressures: a prospective and consequential change in the prevailing balance of power that, even if it comes about by purely accidental reasons, has the effect of upsetting the status quo, creating a disequilibrium that invites collective efforts to either exploit it or ward off its worst consequences.

Tipping events. The second factor consists of specific "tipping events" that can galvanize a group into political action. Tipping events are simply any conspicuous public events that arouse group sensibilities, reinforce beliefs in their insular identity, and set off escalating spirals of mutual expectations about collective resistance to the established order. By their occurrence, they "confirm or justify the [latent] fears or hatreds in[to] a [more] generalized belief; they may initiate or exaggerate a condition of strain; or they may redefine sharply the conditions of conduciveness [leading to future mobilization and violence]."[49] Tipping events can take various forms. They could include large-scale public violence directed at members of a particular group, the destruction of important properties valued by a community, the forcible relocation, banishment, exile, or execution of important or numerous individuals in a community, or any other such *conspicuous* event that induces or reinforces a differential perception of vulnerability. When viewed in retrospect, tipping events of this sort often turn out to become important elements of the historical memory, deepening group identity and accentuating the processes of group formation. They come to serve as the *manifest* symbols of alienation and become "salience indicators"[50] toward which individual fears, resentment, and anger all converge—ready to be either molded by interested elites or exploited by interested factions both within the state and outside it.

Leadership. While "tipping events" can intensify the background conditions for political mobilization and are helpful for that purpose, they are not as essential for ethnic mobilization as the third factor—

---

[49]Neil Smelser, *A Theory of Collective Behavior,* New York: Free Press, 1962, p. 17.

[50]The notion of salience indicators was first developed in Thomas Schelling, *The Strategy of Conflict,* New York: Oxford University Press, 1963, pp. 98ff.

identity entrepreneurs—usually is. "Identity entrepreneurs"[51] are simply individuals who, for self-interested reasons, find it profitable to contribute to creating group identities and bear the costs of mobilizing such groups for political action. Identity entrepreneurs usually rise from within the ranks of a given substatal affinity, but such attachments are not critical, though probably likely when the mobilization is an ethnic one. These entrepreneurs are generally indispensable for group mobilization because of the problems associated with collective action.[52] Such problems usually derive from the fact that any collective action, whether it be engaging in street protests, mobilizing community action, or orchestrating mass resistance against "outsiders" or the state, is invariably characterized by what has been called "the de facto impossibility of exclusion."[53] This means that it is impossible to prevent the entire set of relevant people from consuming the fruits of a particular collective action, even though only a few may have contributed to its production. For example, a protest action against discrimination mounted by a few individuals may create a political windfall that can be enjoyed by other dominated individuals who did not participate in the original protest. Ethnically driven collective actions are, thus, one more example of such collective goods.

Since the ascriptive tradition of viewing ethnicity regards all ethnic groups as composed ultimately of self-interested, or egoistic, individuals, collective goods—like ethnically based social action—either will not be produced in normal circumstances or at best will be produced only in suboptimal "quantities." The deficit in the production of such goods does not arise because collective ethnic mobilization is judged to be *unnecessary* in the face of some palpable deprivation, but only because each individual ethnic agent has great incentives to be a "free rider." Knowing that he cannot be excluded from eventually enjoying the fruits of successful ethnic action, he has few incentives to make an individual contribution to its success. This is be-

---

[51]The term "identity entrepreneur" has been borrowed from Barbara Ballis Lal, "Identity Entrepreneurs: Do We Want Them/Do We Need Them?" unpublished manuscript.

[52]The *locus classicus* for understanding this issue is Mancur Olson, Jr., *The Logic of Collective Action,* Cambridge: Harvard University Press, 1965.

[53]Russell Hardin, *Collective Action,* Baltimore: Johns Hopkins, 1982, p. 20.

cause he judges his own personal contribution to be either insignificant to the success of the final outcome or not worth the costs he will bear in the process of bringing that outcome about. Consequently, every individual ethnic agent is—in the language of game theory—tempted to "defect" when he has to make good on his individual contribution to collective social action.[54] The effect of every individual agent's reasoning this way soon leads to the demise of any possible ethnic action, *even though such action may be both universally recognized as necessary and desired by all individuals sharing certain substatal affinities.*

While it is certainly true that this paradox of "missing" action arises primarily because of a particular view of individual rationality, it is also true that this conception of rationality is sufficiently accurate to describe the motivational structure of most individuals in modern, if not all, societies. Corroborating evidence for this assertion can be seen in the fact that several important collective goods like clean air and public safety cannot be produced except through the intervention of *command* mechanisms like the state. In the case of ethnic mobilization, the state is unavailable as a catalyst and may in fact be an adversary. An alternative mechanism of mobilization is therefore required, and identity entrepreneurs usually fit the bill neatly. Identity entrepreneurs help to resolve the collective action problems in several ways.[55]

To begin with, they can help to "create" the ethnic group—if the group is merely a latent formation up to that point—by "conscientizing" individuals to support certain collective goals as defined by the entrepreneur. This attempt at defining goals for the purpose of mobilizing a given populace is clearly rational and self-interested behavior by the entrepreneur because it aims at enticing individuals to commit themselves and their resources to political actions that advance the entrepreneur's current and future political interests. However, if individuals are as rational and self-regarding as the ascriptive tradition assumes, they would *not* advance the en-

---

[54]Russell Hardin, "Collective Action as an Agreeable *n*-Prisoners' Dilemma," *Behavioral Science*, Vol. 16 (1971), pp. 472–481.

[55]Richard Wagner, "Pressure Groups and Political Entrepreneurs," *Papers in Non-Market Decision-Making*, Vol. 1 (1966), pp. 161–170.

trepreneur's interest by participating in such collective action because, other things being equal, they could gamble on being able to enjoy these goods for free after they have been created. Since the costs accruing to each individual participant would certainly be greater than the benefits accruing to each individually, individual nonparticipation in the face of exhortations by identity entrepreneurs is just as rational as nonparticipation in the context of other calls for community mobilization—precisely the problem that gave rise to a need for identity entrepreneurs in the first place.

This problem can be solved in several ways. One solution would rely on positing that the identity entrepreneur is a very effective purveyor of "false consciousness." In effect, the political entrepreneur is seen in this instance as exercising great "charismatic leadership" in the Weberian sense. As such, he is attributed the capacity to mobilize sentiments and to provide a coherence to the life and actions of individuals in a way that the prevailing social order and the raw fact of latent affinity cannot. The charisma of such leaders serves to suspend the normal calculative rationality of individuals who, putting aside conventional considerations of costs and benefits, tap into their reservoir of extrarational motivations to participate in collective actions despite their potentially high personal cost. While identity entrepreneurs can certainly mobilize collective action by sheer dint of personality in this way, it must be recognized that this process is explicitly extrarational from the ascriptive perspective. It can account for how collective actions originate—activated emotions that almost imply a fit of absence of mind—but it is a relatively precarious explanation for why collective actions sustain themselves over time, because charismatic authority is unstable, often transient, and eventually of limited duration simply because of the mortality of individuals.[56]

An alternative solution to the problem also centers on identity entrepreneurs but runs a more rationalist course. This variant posits that the identity entrepreneur belongs to a "privileged group,"[57] that

---

[56]The limitations of charisma as an explanatory concept have been explored in William Spinrod, "Charisma: A Blighted Concept and an Alternative Formula," *Political Science Quarterly*, Vol. 106, No. 2 (1991), pp. 295–311.

[57]The phrase "privileged group" comes from Olson, op. cit., pp. 49–52.

is, a subgroup with a vested interest in seeing the collective action succeed and willing for purely self-interested reasons to bear the costs of ensuring such success. The self-interested reasons may be political, as is the case when certain individuals perceive that organizing a latent group would advance their own claims to wider political power, or it may be economic, as is the case when certain individuals perceive that empowering a latent group would increase their own markets, wealth, or profits. Whatever the reasons, the identity entrepreneur solves the collective action problem in this case not by activating the emotions of individuals and gambling on suspended rationality but by exploiting individual rationality. This is done through the offering of "selective incentives."[58] These selective incentives may be "positive"—when one or more individuals are compensated (in the form of promises of future political power or simply monetary payments) for their role in orchestrating or participating in collective actions—or they may be "negative"—when one or more individuals are simply coerced into participating in collective actions by threats to their life, liberty, or property. Which sort of selective incentive (or combination thereof) is offered in any given case depends on the character and objectives of the identity entrepreneur in question. What is important, however, is that the mechanism of selective incentives *can* solve the collective action problem in a direct and rational way by introducing excludability ("those who don't participate don't get compensated" or "those who don't participate better watch out") and by equalizing the asymmetry between individual costs and gains ("there are direct benefits for individual participants, not simply diffused gains from future group victories" or "there is special pain for each individual nonparticipant, not simply general discomfort from being quietly worse off").

Because of the solutions embodied by identity entrepreneurs, they become very important for transforming individuals sharing certain affinities into mobilized political groups pursuing certain power-political goals. Given the kinds of techniques they can utilize for this purpose, identity entrepreneurs in particular and ethnic political leadership in general can be seen to arise in one or more of three ways. They may arise from "patrimonial" structures, which is leadership derived from traditional forms of status and power, both eco-

---

[58]Ibid., p. 133.

nomic and political, as held by certain privileged families; they may arise out of "bureaucratic" institutions, which is leadership based on special occupational competency and derived from certain training in civil or religious administration or military affairs; or they may arise out of the dynamic personality characteristics and proclivities of an individual.

Resources and organization. Political leadership in the form of identity entrepreneurs is a necessary catalyst but needs to be supplemented by additional components for effective group mobilization. These additional components are summarized by the fourth factor—resources and organization[59]—in Figure A.1. Both elements are critical. A group's access to resources is in many ways the lifeblood of the mobilization process. It determines the depth of conscientization that can be undertaken, the level of propaganda and public-relations efforts that must be mounted, the kinds of selective incentives that can be offered to bystanders, and, overall, the kind of strategy that the mobilized group can pursue vis-à-vis other competing social formations and the state. For all these reasons, identity entrepreneurs arising out of patrimonial structures will invest their own resources in the movement, while those entrepreneurs arising out of bureaucratic institutions and personality dispositions will have to rely on the resources of others for sustaining the groups they seek to mobilize.

Access to resources can come in many forms: besides personal wealth and family connections, which are usually associated with patrimonial structures, identity entrepreneurs can direct persuasive or coercive efforts at mobilizing internal community resources, seeking contributions from wealthy ethnic cohorts and appealing to ethnic émigrés abroad or to foreign states. The success at mobilizing such resources in all instances will be determined by the following: the levels of wealth within the group; the confidence individuals have in the existing leadership or the effectiveness of the coercive threats mounted by the entrepreneur; the skill in creating domestic and external coalitions; and the extent and intensity of the deprivation felt by the group at large.

---

[59]These factors are most clearly emphasized in the "resource mobilization" perspective in Charles Tilly, *From Mobilization to Revolution,* Reading: Addison-Welsey, 1978.

In addition to resources, which provide the lifeblood for effective mobilization, competent organization provides the arteries that channel the lifeblood into effective action. Competent organization is necessary in the presence of all kinds of entrepreneurship. Entrepreneurship deriving from patrimonial structures usually brings along some form of nascent organizational structure in the form of patrimonial bureaucracies, but even this organization has to be endowed with new powers and capabilities if it is to be responsive to the new demands of large-scale political action. Entrepreneurship based on personality disposition or special vocational competency must create organizational structures from scratch or "annex" existing organizational structures and then orient them to the new goals of ethnic mobilization. These organizational structures are generally needed because communities that have no hierarchic structure and no functional role differentiation are generally ineffective as agents of *large-scale* social mobilization. For such purposes, a formal organizational structure is required. The structure must be capable of carrying out a variety of actions designed to advance the cause sought by the mobilized groups and, as such, would have the following three characteristics.

First, it would have a set of closed relationships at the core, meaning that admission to "outsiders" would be proscribed at least at the level of executive authority. The organization may support open structures like a political party, pressure groups, research and educational institutions, and a legal defense arm, but at its core policymaking level, an ethnically mobilized political group is characterized by a closed organization. Second, the organization also will be autonomous and autocephalous, meaning that it frames its own regulations and takes its orders from its own leaders on their personal (or through bureaucratically mediated) authority and not from outsiders, no matter how well intentioned; further, it regulates issues of leadership, functional roles, and succession through internal means alone. Third, it will focus special attention on ensuring the security of its leadership and the cadres as well as on preserving the sanctity of the channels of communication linking these entities.

Because political mobilization is oriented to altering the relations of power, the ethnic organization must be attentive to both the balance of power among various groups (and the state) as well as to general perceptions of that balance. Toward that end, it must have the capability of countering those forces that would oppose continued mobilization and enticing those elements that adopt a position of neutrality. Achieving such objectives requires a variety of tactics, the most important of which are successful differential mobilization of resources, intelligence about opponent groups, and information warfare. The success of each of these operations is crucially dependent on preserving the security of the leadership-cadre link and the inviolability of the group's means of intelligence gathering, data fusion, and transmission of orders.

The foreign element. The final catalyst for effective mobilization of ethnic groups is the possibility of foreign assistance.[60] In a strict sense, foreign aid to a mobilizing ethnic group is simply another facet of its effort to muster resources. Because it pushes domestic power struggles into the area of interstate competition, however, the role of foreign agencies and states requires separate categorization. The possibility of external assistance to incipiently mobilizing ethnic groups becomes relevant for two reasons. First, state boundaries often do not coincide with the location of ethnic populations. As a result, members of a certain group mobilizing for power within a given country are often tempted to look for assistance from their cohorts located in other states. Such cohorts may occasionally seek to provide tangible support even if it has not been requested by the mobilizing group. Ethnic émigrés abroad are one special case of such possibilities. Second, because interstate competition continues unabated even as domestic struggles for power proceed within states, states may often find it convenient to support domestic challengers abroad simply for purposes of wearing down their competitors. Such support can come in the form of sanctuary for ethnic elites, financial assistance, diplomatic support, provision of organizational expertise, and even covert arms transfers and military training. Because of the serious and extended nature of such interactions, domestic ethnic mobilization may become swiftly enmeshed in the vicissitudes of international politics. The bottom line, therefore, is that foreign support may be critical for the success of ethnic mobilization, and fears

[60]For a good survey of these issues, see Alexis Heraclides, "Secessionist Minorities and External Involvement," *International Organization,* Vol. 44 (1990), pp. 341–378, and K. M. de Silva and R. J. May (eds.), *Internationalization of Ethnic Conflict,* New York: St. Martin's Press, 1991.

of such support often become critical precipitants of intrastate violence as state authorities are tempted to attempt "preemptive strikes" at an ethnic leadership if consequential foreign support appears imminent or likely. A whole set of issues arises in such situations, as the state authorities then can portray the mobilized ethnic group as a foreign agent and, in turn, claim support from their own allies abroad.

Summarizing the logic of mobilization. The purpose of examining the factors that can aid or hinder mobilization is to identify the variables responsible for catalyzing existing latent dissatisfaction into visible political action. When existing differential deprivation is married to the appearance of five factors—the appearance of incipient changes, the existence of tipping events, the rise of identity entrepreneurs, the availability of resources and the development of competent organization, and the potential for foreign assistance—the *potential* for strife moves toward *likelihood.* Whether strife actually occurs, however, does not depend just on the capabilities of the mobilized group. The capabilities and actions of the prevailing stakeholders, namely the state, are crucial as well, and it is to these variables that attention must now turn.

STAGE III

From Likely to Actual Strife: Understanding State Capabilities and the Process of Strategic Bargaining

The possibility of actual strife is always determined by the results of the interaction between the preferences, capabilities, and actions of both the mobilized group and the prevailing stakeholders, namely, the state. The state, it is generally assumed, tends to be more powerful (in an absolute sense) than any single challenger. This perception usually derives from the fact that the state is supposed to possess, in popular conceptions, a monopoly on the means of violence. If this were true in the literal sense of the phrase, the challenge of ethnic strife would be both trivial and uninteresting: trivial because the state would employ its "monopoly" on force to readily crush any incipient challenge by a substatal group, and uninteresting because all assessments of possible ethnic strife would be little more than a narrative of abortive and failed challenges.

The empirical record, however, suggests that this is not the case. Communal challenges, including ethnic groups, do sometimes succeed, and this is due to the fact that the state—both in theory and in practice—never enjoys a *real* monopoly on the use of force. Weber understood this well enough, and for that reason described the state as an institution that merely lays *claim* to the monopoly of *legitimate* violence within a territory. Mobilizing groups, therefore, stand a chance when contending with state power because the state, just like other social formations, is constantly struggling to dominate various nodes that generate power within a given society, even as it constantly seeks to increase the levels of coercive power it has available, but by no means monopolizes. The mobilized group, then, has certain advantages in that it is never confronted by a "state" that is a single unitary actor with a monopoly on social resources, including the capacity for violence, and therein lie precisely the possibilities for successfully pressing certain political claims.[61]

Understanding how this process can unfold requires an understanding of the nature of the state. The state, simply put, is first and foremost a security-producing *institution.* As such, it involves a territorially defined set of political relationships. These relationships, which take the form of a hierarchy based on coercion and sustained by some concentration of force, are intended primarily for the protection of the dominant elites at the apex but provide, as an unintended consequence, relative safety for the subordinated subjects further down the coercive chain.[62]

This implies that the state, far from being a simple unitary organism, has many "parts." These include the dominant elites at the apex of the institutional structure who "rule" the polity. Below them are several bureaucracies consisting of the army, police, intelligence agencies, tax collectors, and propagandists. The task of such bureaucracies is to maintain security and order with a view to preserving the prevailing structure of power and to effectively collect the revenues required from civil society with a view to both sustaining the struc-

[61]For an insightful analysis, see Gordon Tullock, *The Social Dilemma: The Economics of War and Revolution,* Blacksburg: University Publications, 1974.

[62]This formulation is amplified and its consequences explored in Ashley J. Tellis, *The Drive to Domination: Towards a Pure Realist Theory of Politics,* unpublished Ph.D. dissertation, The University of Chicago, 1994, pp. 257–285.

tures for power and undertaking redistributional and welfare functions more generally. Finally, there is civil society itself, which consists of ordinary citizens existing atomistically as well as in the form of other large-scale economic organizations like industrial enterprises, agricultural combines, universities, and the like.[63]

Since these formal arrangements mask more invisible patterns of distributed power and wealth, the task of the state essentially boils down to either preserving the existing exclusionary patterns of closure in the polity or preventing the usurpationary attempts at changing existing power relations from manifesting themselves through violence. In effect, therefore, the dominant elites who "rule" the state seek to use the multiple bureaucracies either to preserve their own power or, in more accommodative political systems, to prevent the incipient changes in power relations from taking place through violent means.

But since the ascriptive tradition assumes that all individuals in the system are rational and egoistic, it is evident that the state too faces multiple kinds of collective-action problems as elites attempt to maneuver their underlings to confront the mobilized communal or ethnic groups seeking political change. In the strictest sense, the collective-action problem facing these ruling elites is identical to that facing identity entrepreneurs at the opposite end: to mobilize a group of individuals to undertake a certain task that imposes higher individual costs on each of them in comparison to their individually realized benefits. At the state's end, however, the issue may not be getting individuals to rally behind calls for redistributing certain resources—which, for example, is the problem confronting the identity entrepreneur—but rather to find a way to induce numerous citizens to do a variety of individually burdensome tasks, as represented by the challenges facing policemen confronting unruly mobs, armies tasked with hunting down armed resisters, and tax collectors responsible for levying assessments on a recalcitrant populace. In every such instance, the problem remains the same: for the agents undertaking these tasks, the individual burdens are greater than the

[63]For a useful survey of the current state of research on the state as a political structure and on the nature of rule, see Theda Skocpol, "Bringing the State Back In: Strategies of Analysis in Current Research," in Peter B. Evans et al. (eds.), *Bringing the State Back In*, Cambridge: Cambridge University Press, 1985, pp. 3–37.

individual benefits, so each is inclined to avoid contributing in the expectation that he could enjoy all the benefits as long as someone else contributed in his stead.

Precisely to avoid such collective-action problems, state managers do not rely on a collection of atomistic agents but rather structure these agents into a hierarchically ordered organization. Such an organization enables both systematic monitoring of individual action and the efficient coupling of such actions to a structured system of rewards and penalties, thus enabling state managers to extract the desired behavior from what is otherwise merely a large mass of individual actors. The system of rewards and penalties serves to help equalize the disparity between individual costs and benefits facing each agent, though it can never quite equalize these values entirely. For this reason, embedded rules, norms, and expectations of good behavior are developed as part of an organizational "ethos." This organizational ethos serves to provide psychic benefits which, in turn, help to reduce the costs of individual action still further, thus bringing them closer to the level of individually realized benefits.

As an *ultima ratio*, however, action by an individual agent is ensured simply by means of sanctions, which in the extreme may involve the taking of life. This enforcement of sanctions, too, is embodied in a transitive system in which each individual complies with his duties because there is another to punish him, still another to punish the punisher, and so on. In a simple sense, then, the state is effective (in the sense of being able to compel agents to perform their duties) because the monarch or the ruling elite serve as the "ultimate punishers," as used to be the case in traditional kingdoms ruled by free, physically strong, rulers.[64] As modern political theory has demonstrated, however, even if such an asymmetrically powerful "omega point" does not exist, agents can still be made to carry out extremely (individually) hazardous orders. Such compliance ensues not because of fear of some omnipotent sovereign (who may not exist), but because each agent, fearing that another (or some others) may obey the existing authority, rushes to obey first. The net result of this logic, where each agent obeys because of fear that some other(s) might obey, allows state elites to secure the compliance of subordi-

[64]J. R. Lucas, *The Principles of Politics,* Oxford: Clarendon Press, 1985, p. 76.

nate agents, despite the fact that these elites may actually be weaker than any given subset of the subordinate population imaginable.[65]

The state, therefore, can solve its collective-action problem, though not assuredly or in every instance. In that sense, it only mirrors the problems faced by an incipiently mobilizing group that may be successful on some occasions but not on others. In any event, however, the capacity of the state will be determined by its ability to successfully undertake not one but two kinds of countermobilization in the face of an emerging ethnic opposition group. First, it has to be able to mobilize its own bureaucracies to undertake a range of direct—immediate—actions against the group, if necessary. Second, and only a trifle less urgently, it must be able to mobilize important sections of civil society, especially critical co-ethnic groups or class formations whose support is essential for the preservation of the existing systems of closure. Here, the state could use its bureaucracies to coerce civil society into providing it with the resources and support necessary for its confrontation with the newly mobilized ethnic group, but such actions do not augur well for the possibility of effectively containing the larger problem.[66]

In any event, a state's capacity to cope with its new "demands groups" is a function of its strength along three dimensions, and each of these must be briefly described as the first step toward understanding how likely strife may be transformed into actual strife. This preliminary step, which consists simply of investigating the nature, extent, and depth of state capabilities, is analogous to the previous step of establishing the requirements for successful ethnic mobilization: it completes the story about the required capabilities of the antagonists. Once these state capabilities are explored, it is possible to understand the nature of feasible state responses because this latter set is bounded critically by both the nature of abstract state preferences and its existing capabilities.

The first step—understanding state capabilities—therefore requires an examination of the three constitutive facets of state power,

---

[65]For formal proof of this proposition, see Tellis, op. cit., pp. 288–309.

[66]See the discussion in Jeff Goodwin and Theda Skocpol, "Explaining Revolutions in the Contemporary Third World," in Theda Skocpol, *Social Revolutions in the Modern World*, New York: Cambridge University Press, 1994, pp. 28–31.

namely its accommodative capacity as defined by its political structure, its fiscal capability as measured by the health of its treasury, and its coercive capability, which refers to its ability and willingness to use effective force.

The accommodative capability of the state is probably the most important variable for the purposes of anticipating ethnic violence, since, as argued earlier, ethnic movements are simply special forms of political movements struggling for power. Given this fact, the most important issue for the state is its institutional structure or, in other words, its structured capacity for responsiveness to the demands of its constituents. This variable is, in turn, a function of two specific dimensions: the level of inclusion as expressed by the character of the regime, and the nature of organizational design that enables or retards the possibility of peaceful change. The nature of the established political structure, then, combines with the prevailing norms of governance and the cohesion of the ruling elites to determine the accommodative capacity of a given state. This varies as well, and democratic, oligarchic, and authoritarian states will exhibit a variety of different capacities in this regard.

The fiscal capacity of the state is the next important variable for purposes of anticipating ethnic violence because it relates, among other things, to the issue of how a state can ameliorate the demands of mobilized groups short of using force. Clearly, the use of this capacity is dependent on the character of the political regime to begin with, but it warrants independent analysis because it identifies the margins of maneuver that a state has irrespective of its political structure. Three components are relevant in this regard: (1) the overall condition of the state treasury, meaning the extent of existing surpluses and deficits and the prevailing and prospective composition of budgetary expenditures; (2) the state's potential extractive capacity, meaning the capacity to extract additional revenues without fear of accentuating political resistance; and (3) the extent and durability of its social base, meaning the size and wealth of the class base supporting the existing ruling elites.

The coercive capacity of the state is the final variable for the purposes of anticipating ethnic violence because it relates, in the final analysis, to the state's ability to conclusively attempt suppression of political mobilization by force. This variable is ranked third not because of its lesser importance but because coercion is generally understood to be the ultimate arbiter of rule, though many regimes use coercion quite effectively as the means of first *and* last resort. In any event, the relevant components in this connection are (1) the structural relationship between the ruling elites and the bureaucracies of violence; (2) the social composition of the external and internal security organs; (3) the state's reputation for the use of force, which incorporates historical tradition, attitudes, and experience with respect to the use of force[67]; and (4) the technical capability of the external and internal security forces for purposes of suppressing unrest.

These state capabilities writ large describe in effect its latent capacity to offset popular mobilization by a group challenging the current ruling elites. As such, they represent the state's "assets" (or liabilities, as the case may be) in the interaction with various challenging groups. In contrast to the levels of deprivation and possibilities of mobilization, which represent the "demand" side of the equation relating to probable ethnic violence, the state's capabilities in the accommodative, fiscal, and coercive dimensions then represent the "supply" side.

Having completed this examination of state capacity, it is now possible to embark on the second step of Stage III, which consists of investigating the nature of the strategic bargaining that ensues between the mobilized group and the state. This requires systematically matching up the feasible preferences, alternative capabilities, and potential actions of both the mobilized ethnic group and the state to discover the range of possible social outcomes. Because this model attempts to assist the analyst tasked with intelligence and warning, and is for that reason fundamentally a conceptual effort to understand the prospect for ethnic violence long before it materializes, the objective of the following section is not to provide accurate "point predictions" of when ethnic violence will occur but rather to structure thought about how combinations of group and state preferences and capabilities interact to produce a variety of political con-

[67]Empirical studies have shown a 5–7 year "memory" of democratic and nonrepressive norms that affect negatively the use of force by the state. Christian Davenport, "The Weight of the Past: Exploring Lagged Determinants of Political Repression," *Political Research Quarterly*, Vol. 49, No. 2 (June 1996), pp. 377–403.

sequences, ranging from political reconciliation to state breakdown. Because some of these consequences embody strife in varying forms and intensity, they provide a means of "backward deduction," that is, they allow the analyst to discover which combinations of group/state preferences and capabilities are particularly volatile. If such preferences and capabilities are then seen to materialize in any given case of communal action, the intelligence analysts can "flag" that case as potentially troublesome. Such cases warrant closer scrutiny by other crisis assessment or "watch" teams, and may even justify preemptive political intervention if these strife-prone areas are of importance to the United States.

Before this process of strategic bargaining is modeled, it is worth mentioning that such a straightforward dyadic interaction between group and state represents only one, and is in fact the simplest, kind of encounter that can be envisaged. A more complex situation, and perhaps one that has greater empirical fidelity to the real world, would involve not simply one ethnic group facing the state but rather one ethnic group facing perhaps several others in addition to confronting the state. The origins of such situations are themselves very interesting. The successful mobilization of one ethnic group may in fact give rise to successful competitive mobilization on the part of other groups, and ethnic competition in such instances may arise not only because the less advantaged group embarks on "usurpationary" closure but also because the more advantaged group feels compelled to preemptively reinforce existing "exclusionary" patterns of closure in order to stave off a potentially successful challenge to their privileges.[68] Irrespective of the immediate causes of ethnic competition (or for that matter their more remote origins), the fact remains that modeling the processes of strategic bargaining in situations where there are more than two entities remains a very challenging task.

This difficulty is only compounded by the fact that the number of entities in play increases when the state is factored in as a relevant actor. In fact, in situations where multiple ethnic groups exist in some relationship of super- and subordination among themselves, the relationship of the state to the various mobilized groups becomes

---

[68]The dynamics of such actions are explored in Barry Posen, "The Security Dilemma and Ethnic Conflict," *Survival*, Vol. 35 (Spring 1993), pp. 27–67.

a critical factor conditioning the extent of the latter's success. The degree of autonomy enjoyed by the state from its social bases of power, in conjunction with its own inherent capabilities, will determine whether the state plays the role of an umpire between various contending groups or whether it turns out to be an abettor, if not a direct precipitant, of exclusionary political action. Modeling the state in each of these roles would be desirable if a complete or "intensive" understanding of the processes of strategic bargaining is required. Such modeling, however, would require formal analysis, including the use of mathematical tools, and lies beyond the scope of this preliminary effort.

Finally, a complete analysis of strategic bargaining would require explicitly incorporating the international system as a causal variable. The international environment not only provides possibilities of external support for mobilized social groups within a state, it also affects the extent and character of *internal* state action through the resources it diverts for external power-political purposes. In fact, as much modern research has shown, events pertaining to the external environment like victory or defeat in war often act as a precipitant for the mobilization of various social groups within a country, sometimes on ethnic lines. Consequently, the effect of the external environment—either as efficient or permissive cause—has to be incorporated explicitly into an analysis of strategic bargaining for reasons of completeness.

This section, however, avoids all the aforementioned complications not because of their lack of importance but because of the need for simplicity. Since it aims to establish simply "proof of concept" for the intelligence community and other interested observers, it settles for explicating the simplest case: a dyadic encounter between a single mobilized group and the state. If the ensuing analysis provides a useful tool for conceptualizing the process of strategic bargaining, it will have served its purpose, while also opening the door to future work (perhaps carried out by others) aimed at "intensively" expanding the model through a formal incorporation of more variables like many mobilized groups, the state in multiple roles, and differing opportunities and constraints imposed by the international system.

Given this intention of demarcating the range of outcomes in a simple dyadic encounter between group and state, the process of strategic bargaining is modeled as a three-step process through the means of several tables and matrices. The steps are linked in such a way that the outcomes of a preceding table or matrix become the dimensions on the axis of the following matrix.

The first step involves "measuring" the capacities of both the mobilized group and the state. The capacity of the mobilized group is measured with a view to assessing its ability to be accommodative vis-à-vis other competing social formations, including the state; its ability to sustain the political campaign for redress of its grievances; and its ability to maintain the cohesiveness of its emerging group identity. Based on the earlier discussion of group formation, the group's capacity to be accommodative, to sustain its political aims, and to maintain its cohesion is assessed (strong or weak) in (1) leadership, (2) access to resources and organization, and (3) levels of popular support, respectively.

The full extent of the variations in group capacity are depicted again in binary terms (high-low) in Table A.1.

The principles through which variations in the three categories (leadership, resources, and popular support) lead to specific rankings in the three capacities (accommodative, sustainment, and cohesiveness) are given below.

Principle 1: leadership and accommodative capacity are linked directly, subject to modification according to popular support values.

- 1a. strong leadership = high accommodative capacity, unless it has weak popular support (in such a case, low accommodative capacity)
- 1b. weak leadership = low accommodative capacity, unless it has weak popular support (in such a case, high accommodative capacity)

Principle 2: resource support and sustainment are linked directly, subject to modification according to popular support values.

- 2a. good resource support = high sustainment capacity, unless it has weak popular support (in such a case, low sustainment capacity)
- 2b. weak resource support = low sustainment capacity

Principle 3: popular support and cohesiveness capacity are linked directly, subject to modification according to leadership values.

3a. broad popular support = high cohesiveness capacity, unless it has weak leadership (in such a case, low cohesiveness capacity)

3b. weak popular support = low cohesiveness capacity

Table A.1

Capacity of a Mobilized Group

Type of Mobilized Group		Capacity		
Code	Descriptors	Accommodative	Sustainment	Cohesiveness
A	Strong leadership Good resource support Broad popular support	High	High	High
B	Weak leadership Good resource support Broad popular support	Low	High	Low
C	Strong leadership Weak resource support Broad popular support	High	Low	High
D	Strong leadership Good resource support Weak popular support	Low	High	High
E	Weak leadership Weak resource support Broad popular support	Low	Low	Low
F	Weak leadership Weak resource support Weak popular support	High	Low	Low
G	Strong leadership Weak resource support Weak popular support	Low	Low	Low
H	Weak leadership Good resource support Weak popular support	Low	High	Low

The capacity of the state is measured in similar (though not identical) areas. Based on previous discussion, again, the process seeks to assess—specifically—the state's capacity to accommodate the group's demands; its ability to sustain its own political preferences vis-à-vis the mobilized group; and finally, its ability to coerce its opponents in the first or last resort depending on the nature of the state in question. To assess these capacities, three variables are interrogated, again in binary terms: these include the strength of the ruling elites (strong-weak); the vitality of the fiscal base (strong-weak); and the overall character of the political structure (exclusionary-inclusionary).

The full extent of the variations in state capacity are depicted, again in binary terms (high-low), in Table A.2.

The principles through which variations in the three categories (leadership, fiscal position, and type of regime) lead to specific rankings in the three capacities (accommodative, sustainment, and coercive) are given below.

Principle 1: leadership and accommodative capacity are linked directly, subject to modification according to type of regime and fiscal position values.

1a. strong leadership = high accommodative capacity, unless it is an exclusive regime (in such a case, low accommodative capacity)

1b. weak leadership = low accommodative capacity, unless it is an inclusive regime and a weak fiscal position (in such a case, high accommodative capacity)

Principle 2: fiscal position and sustainment are linked directly.

2a. strong fiscal position = high sustainment capacity

2b. weak fiscal position = low sustainment capacity

Principle 3: type of regime and coercive capacity are linked directly, subject to modification according to leadership values.

3a. inclusive regime = low coercive capacity

3b. exclusive regime = high coercive capacity, unless it has weak leadership (in such a case, low coercive capacity)

Table A.2

Capacity of the State

Type of State		Capacity		
Code	Descriptors	Accommodative	Sustainment	Coercive
A	Strong leadership Strong fiscal position Inclusive regime	High	High	Low
B	Weak leadership Strong fiscal position Inclusive regime	Low	Low	High
C	Strong leadership Weak fiscal position Inclusive regime	High	Low	Low
D	Strong leadership Strong fiscal position Exclusive regime	Low	Low	High
E	Weak leadership Weak fiscal position Inclusive regime	High	Low	Low
F	Weak leadership Weak fiscal position Exclusive regime	Low	Low	Low
G	Strong leadership Weak fiscal position Exclusive regime	Low	Low	High
H	Weak leadership Strong fiscal position Exclusive regime	Low	High	High

The preferences of both group and state are measured, thereafter, on the implicit premise that the nature of an entity's effective capacity would determine its revealed preference. To be sure, the causal logic may run in the opposite direction in some instances, but such anomalies are not considered because they would be difficult to model (thanks to their inherent indeterminacy) and, more important, because such anomalies would not survive very long if there was a radical disjunction between the preferred objectives/strategies and the underlying capacity to secure/sustain these ends. On the premise that capacity therefore drives preferences, each entity is allowed a choice of four options: The mobilized group can choose between negotiation, exploitation, intimidation, or surrender, and the first three choices in every given situation are rank ordered. The state, in turn, can choose between negotiation, exploitation, repression, or surrender.

Since these strategic choices cannot be identified in the abstract but only in the context of specifically profiled groups facing specifically profiled states, the logical (and probable) choices of both group and state are arranged in matrix form. That is, the preferences of every conceivable type of group—created as a result of comprehensive variation in the kind of leadership, levels of resources, and extent of popular support (sketched in Table A.1)—are rank ordered (down to three levels) on the basis of their respective capacities (sketched in Table A.1) in the context of hypothetical confrontations with every conceivable type of state.

The principles governing the preference focus on the leadership capacity as the dynamic driving force behind group actions, though they are subject to modification based on the other two factors. The principles governing the mobilized group preferences are

1. A strong group leadership faced with a strong state leadership will have a preference for negotiation with an inclusive regime.
2. A strong group leadership faced with a weak state leadership usually will have a preference to exploit or intimidate the latter depending on other factors (coercive/cohesive values).
3. A weak group leadership faced with a strong state leadership usually will have a preference for exploitation, but will opt for intimidation or negotiation depending on other factors (resources).
4. A weak group leadership faced with a weak state leadership will almost always opt for exploitation or intimidation, particularly if the former has weak popular support or if the latter is an exclusive regime.

Based on the choices arrived at through such rules, the range of group preferences is demarcated in Matrix A.1.

A similar exercise is undertaken for the state. The preferences of every conceivable kind of state—created as a result of comprehensive variation in the kind of leadership, vitality of resource base, and level of inclusiveness in political structure (sketched in Table A.2)—are rank ordered (down to three levels) on the basis of their respective capacities (sketched in Table A.2) in the context of hypothetical confrontations with every conceivable type of group.[69]

Just as in the case of the group, the principles governing the preferences focus on the leadership capacity as the dynamic driving force behind state actions, though they are subject to modification based on the other two factors.

The principles governing the state preferences are

1. A strong state leadership faced with a strong group leadership usually will have a preference for negotiation unless it is an exclusive regime or the group has weak popular or resource support, in which case it will repress.
2. A strong state leadership faced with a weak group leadership usually will have a preference to exploit its advantage but may try to repress if the group has weak popular support or to negotiate if it has broad popular support.

---

[69]The decision rules for rank ordering derive from an assessment of the relative strength in various dimensions of state capacity—accommodation, sustainment, and coercion—informed by a judgment of state behavior drawn from public choice theory. Since the process of strategic bargaining is part and parcel of the larger processes of political competition, it is logical to assume that securing, holding on to, and eventually augmenting one's political power is the ultimate "prize" of the competition. Consequently, it is reasonable to assume decision rules of the following kind: all state leaders will divest economic power before they divest themselves of political power. That is, access to wealth is *relatively* less important than determining and enforcing "the rules of the game." Whether state elites will attempt to coerce first or open the level of access to political rule-making and enforcement will be determined by the nature of the political structures in question. That is, exclusionary political systems (defined as such both by ethos and institutional design) will attempt to coerce political opponents *before* they give up extant power, whereas more inclusionary political systems will divest control of rule-making and enforcement before they attempt to coerce political opponents. There is, however, a crucial caveat: in *all* cases, existing state elites will attempt to coerce political opponents *before* they give up extant power, if the mobilized groups are seen to be beneficiaries of effective foreign assistance, since in all these cases the struggle over internal stratification intersects uncomfortably with the demands of interstate competition. This latter rule is not reflected in the matrices, but should be kept in mind.

Matrix A.1

Mobilized Group Preferences

Mobilized Group Type (Table A.1)	State Type (Table A.2)							
	A	B	C	D	E	F	G	H
A	1. Neg 2. Exp 3. Int	1. Exp 2. Int 3. Neg	1. Neg 2. Exp 3. Int	1. Int 2. Exp 3. Neg	1. Neg 2. Exp 3. Int	1. Exp 2. Int 3. Neg	1. Int 2. Exp 3. Neg	1. Exp 2. Int 3. Neg
B	1. Exp 2. Int 3. Neg	1. Int 2. Exp 3. Neg	1. Neg 2. Exp 3. Int	1. Int 2. Neg 3. Int	1. Int 2. Exp 3. Neg	1. Int 2. Exp 3. Neg	1. Exp 2. Neg 3. Int	1. Exp 2. Int 3. Neg
C	1. Neg 2. Exp 3. Int	1. Exp 2. Neg 3. Int	1. Neg 2. Exp 3. Int	1. Int 2. Neg 3. Exp	1. Exp 2. Int 3. Neg	1. Int 2. Exp 3. Neg	1. Int 2. Exp 3. Neg	1. Exp 2. Int 3. Neg
D	1. Neg 2. Exp 3. Int	1. Exp 2. Neg 3. Int	1. Neg 2. Exp 3. Int	1. Int 2. Exp 3. Neg	1. Int 2. Exp 3. Int	1. Int 2. Exp 3. Neg	1. Exp 2. Neg 3. Int	1. Exp 2. Neg 3. Int
E	1. Exp 2. Neg 3. Int	1. Exp 2. Int 3. Neg	1. Exp 2. Neg 3. Int	1. Exp 2. Neg 3. Int	1. Exp 2. Int 3. Neg	1. Int 2. Exp 3. Neg	1. Neg 2. Exp 3. Sur	1. Exp 2. Int 3. Neg
F	1. Neg 2. Exp 3. Sur	1. Exp 2. Neg 3. Sur	1. Neg 2. Exp 3. Int	1. Neg 2. Exp 3. Sur	1. Exp 2. Int 3. Neg	1. Exp 2. Int 3. Neg	1. Exp 2. Neg 3. Sur	1. Exp 2. Int 3. Neg
G	1. Exp 2. Neg 3. Int	1. Int 2. Exp 3. Neg	1. Neg 2. Exp 3. Int	1. Int 2. Neg 3. Exp	1. Int 2. Exp 3. Neg	1. Int 2. Exp 3. Neg	1. Exp 2. Int 3. Neg	1. Int 2. Exp 3. Neg
H	1. Exp 2. Neg 3. Sur	1. Exp 2. Int 3. Neg	1. Exp 2. Int 3. Neg	1. Exp 2. Int 3. Neg	1. Int 2. Exp 3. Neg	1. Int 2. Exp 3. Neg	1. Exp 2. Int 3. Neg	1. Exp 2. Neg 3. Int

Matrix A.2

State Preferences

Mobilized Group Type (Table A.1)	State Type (Table A.2)							
	A	B	C	D	E	F	G	H
A	1. Neg 2. Exp 3. Rep	1. Neg 2. Exp 3. Rep	1. Neg 2. Exp 3. Rep	1. Rep 2. Neg 3. Rep	1. Neg 2. Exp 3. Sur	1. Rep 2. Exp 3. Neg	1. Rep 2. Exp 3. Neg	1. Exp 2. Rep 3. Neg
B	1. Exp 2. Neg 3. Rep	1. Neg 2. Exp 3. Rep	1. Neg 2. Exp 3. Rep	1. Exp 2. Rep 3. Neg	1. Neg 2. Exp 3. Rep	1. Exp 2. Rep 3. Neg	1. Exp 2. Neg 3. Rep	1. Exp 2. Rep 3. Neg
C	1. Neg 2. Exp 3. Rep	1. Neg 2. Exp 3. Rep	1. Neg 2. Exp 3. Rep	1. Rep 2. Exp 3. Neg	1. Neg 2. Exp 3. Sur	1. Rep 2. Exp 3. Neg	1. Rep 2. Exp 3. Neg	1. Rep 2. Exp 3. Neg
D	1. Rep 2. Neg 3. Exp	1. Neg 2. Rep 3. Exp	1. Rep 2. Exp 3. Neg	1. Rep 2. Exp 3. Neg	1. Neg 2. Exp 3. Rep	1. Rep 2. Exp 3. Neg	1. Rep 2. Exp 3. Neg	1. Rep 2. Exp 3. Neg
E	1. Exp 2. Neg 3. Rep	1. Neg 2. Exp 3. Rep	1. Exp 2. Neg 3. Rep	1. Exp 2. Neg 3. Rep	1. Neg 2. Exp 3. Rep	1. Rep 2. Exp 3. Neg	1. Exp 2. Neg 3. Rep	1. Rep 2. Exp 3. Neg
F	1. Rep 2. Exp 3. Neg	1. Neg 2. Exp 3. Rep	1. Rep 2. Exp 3. Neg	1. Rep 2. Exp 3. Neg	1. Neg 2. Rep 3. Exp	1. Exp 2. Rep 3. Neg	1. Rep 2. Exp 3. Neg	1. Rep 2. Exp 3. Neg
G	1. Rep 2. Neg 3. Exp	1. Neg 2. Exp 3. Rep	1. Rep 2. Exp 3. Neg	1. Rep 2. Exp 3. Neg	1. Neg 2. Exp 3. Rep	1. Rep 2. Exp 3. Neg	1. Rep 2. Exp 3. Neg	1. Exp 2. Rep 3. Neg
H	1. Rep 2. Exp 3. Neg	1. Neg 2. Exp 3. Rep	1. Rep 2. Exp 3. Neg	1. Rep 2. Exp 3. Neg	1. Neg 2. Exp 3. Rep	1. Exp 2. Rep 3. Neg	1. Rep 2. Exp 3. Neg	1. Exp 2. Rep 3. Neg

3. A weak state leadership faced with a strong group leadership usually will have a preference for negotiation or exploitation, particularly if the state is inclusive. If the state is exclusive, it will attempt to exploit or repress before negotiating.
4. A weak state leadership faced with a weak group leadership will usually try to exploit or repress, unless it is inclusive, in which case it will try to negotiate first.

Based on the choices arrived at through such rules, the range of state preferences is demarcated in Matrix A.2.

These two matrices, when viewed synoptically, yield a picture that identifies a wide variety of outcomes, according to a specific group or state type.

But since the propensity for violence is the specific issue of interest here, the combinations that yield violent actions (on either or both sides) should be a special concern for the intelligence analyst, since they identify particularly combustible combinations. An examination of the results (first and second preferences matched together) points to some insights (see Table A.3).

Thus, for example, the rankings here suggest that states that have more exclusionary political structures[70] and groups that have relatively weak popular support appear to have the largest number of first-order preferences that involve violence. If the decision rules governing the choices for states or groups are altered, or if the salience of effective foreign assistance is deliberately factored into the combinations in either of the two matrices, it is possible that the number of outcomes exhibiting violence as a first-order preference may increase.

This research effort has made no attempt to identify all possible outcomes that can be derived by varying the decision rules or integrating ambiguity in the form of nonbinary choices like "neither strong nor weak" or "medium." Incorporating such choices makes the outcomes themselves more ambiguous. This may in fact be a more ac-

---

[70]This finding has been borne out in empirical studies; see Rudolph J. Rummel, "Is Collective Violence Correlated with Social Pluralism?" *Journal of Peace Research*, Vol. 34, No. 2 (1997), pp. 163–175.

curate reflection of what social events look like in practice, but such an effort is not justified by the intentions underlying this theoretical effort. After all, the objective here is not to provide a "ready reckoner" that can render irrelevant the knowledge or judgment of regional analysts, but rather to provide a heuristic device that frames both the understanding of communal mobilization and identifies the kinds of variables that may have a bearing on the choice for violence by the mobilized group or the state. To that degree, this theoretical model must be viewed as a "first cut," an invitation to further research both conceptual and empirical as well as a template that can be further elaborated and embellished.

Table A.3

Characteristics of States and Groups, Ranked According to Their Propensity Toward Violence (1st + 2nd preference)

State Types	
F = 7+1	Weak leadership, Weak fiscal position, Exclusive regime
D = 7+0	Strong leadership, Strong fiscal position, Exclusive regime
G = 6+0	Strong leadership, Weak fiscal position, Exclusive regime
H = 5+3	Weak leadership, Strong fiscal position, Exclusive regime
E = 4+3	Weak leadership, Weak fiscal position, Inclusive regime
A = 4+1	Strong leadership, Strong fiscal position, Inclusive regime
C = 4+0	Strong leadership, Weak fiscal position, Inclusive regime
B = 2+4	Weak leadership, Strong fiscal position, Inclusive regime
Group Types	
G = 8+0	Strong leadership, Weak resources, Weak popular support
D = 7+1	Strong leadership, Good resources, Weak popular support
H = 6+2	Weak leadership, Good resources, Weak popular support
F = 5+2	Weak leadership, Weak resources, Weak popular support
B = 4+2	Weak leadership, Good resources, Broad popular support
C = 4+1	Strong leadership, Weak resources, Broad popular support
A = 3+2	Strong leadership, Good resources, Broad popular support
E = 2+2	Weak leadership, Weak resources, Broad popular support

Conclusion

The theoretical framework and the model presented in this appendix attempt to provide a systematic understanding of the phenomenology of ethnic mobilization and its potential for violence. They serve as the conceptual underpinning for the practical handbook for intelligence analysts dealing with ethnic conflict presented in the main body of this report. The questions listed in the handbook are derived directly or by implication from the substantive arguments presented here. For this reason, it is perhaps appropriate to end with a few words of caution.

This report focused on understanding *one* particular kind of ethnic action: the rise of an ethnic group challenging the state. It did not examine other kinds of ethnic competition, such as those that ensue when several ethnic groups arise more or less simultaneously and in competition with one another (with the state acting either as umpire, abettor, or participant). It also did not examine in any detail ethnic action that arises principally from exclusionary closure (as opposed to usurpationary action). Explaining such phenomena may require other theoretical models based, to some degree or another, on the one offered here. Alternatively, it may be possible to "model" these alternative paths to strife as variant cases of the base model offered in this report. In any event, this requires additional research that may be undertaken in the future. This research effort also did not focus on falsifying the theoretical claims offered here in the context of other alternatives that may exist in the literature. Such work too requires further consideration and effort.